HINDU FASTS, FESTIVALS AND CEREMONIES

HINDU FASTS, FESTIVALS AND CEREMONIES

RAMESH CHANDER DOGRA, MBE
URMILA DOGRA

ADITYA PRAKASHAN
New Delhi

First Published 2008

ISBN 13: 978-81-7742-080-7

Published by Aditya Prakashan, 2/18, Ansari Road, New Delhi – 110 002.
email: contact@adityaprakashan.com
website: www.adityaprakashan.com.

Printed at D.K. Fine Arts, Delhi – 110 052.

Contents

Introduction

Hinduism

It is the world's oldest, most tolerant and peace-loving religion, embracing about 83 per cent of the total population of over a billion in India. Like the term India, the term Hindu is of foreign origin. The people who lived near the river Sindhu were known as the inhabitants of Sindhu, and the Persians, who found difficulty in pronouncing an initial - s, called them Hindu. It embraces the whole of Indian thought from Rig Vedic times (10,000 BC). Hindus describe their religion as eternal (Sanatan). Hinduism is not a religion, as it consists of various faiths by the same pantheon. It has developed a great appetite for absorbing every kind of belief. The Indians believed in both monotheistic (One God) and polytheistic (many gods) i.e., powers of nature (sun, moon, air etc.) and worshipped them through prayers, hymns and sacrifice. Hindus believe in the word Om, an auspicious and most sacred symbol of Hinduism, One Supreme God, the concept of incarnation (Avtar), righteousness, Murti Puja (worship of God through idol). Images are meant only as an aid to meditation and that is why the face and shape of the image changes according to the will of the artist who makes it. Hinduism believes in Ahimsa (non-violence), Truth, Doctrine of Karma (deeds, actions) and four stages of life (studentship, marriage, retreat from married life and renunciation and doing good to others).

Hindu scriptures

The Vedas (10,000 BC) are holy books, which constitute the foundation of Hindu religion. There are four Vedas (Rig, Yajur, Sam and Atharva). Puranas, 18 basic Puranas (old religious literature), 6 Shastras (Sankhya, Yoga, Nyaya, Vaisheshik, Purvamimansa, and Vedanta), Dharama Shastra (Hindu law), Manu Smriti (another law book), Bhagvad-gita (philosophy of life), Ramayana (adventures of Lord Ram) and Mahabharat (longest poem on War for justice and truth).

Fasts, festivals and ceremonies

Fasts forms part of the religious practices in Hinduism. Hindus are very found of celebrations and therefore the whole year is full of fasts and festivals than any other religion. Fasts have religious, social and hygienic elements in them as bathing and prayers are their essential parts. Monday fast is in honor of Lord Shiva or the moon; Tuesday is in honor of Hanuman; Wednesday in honor of Ganesh; Thursday for Saraswati (Goddess of learning); Friday in honor of Shukra Devta and other minor Gods; Saturday for the planet Saturn or the Mother Goddess or Hanuman and Sunday in honor of the Sun or the Mother Goddess. There are many other fasts connected with smaller deities, and a festive occasion may be observed with acts of fasting, worship, bathing etc.

The first purpose of the fast is to obtain by this act of penitence the forgiveness of their sins; and the second to avert the malign influence of the stars; and thirdly to pray for the well being and progress of their family members. A prudential motive may also have originally tended to as conducing to their bodily health.

Festivals

Many festivals are seasonal; some celebrate the harvest or fertility of the fields; some commemorate the birth, inauguration, or victory of a God or hero. Some are dedicated to the phases of the moon, to eclipse, solstices, and equinoxes, to the stars. Some are celebrated in honor of Gods/Goddesses (Krishna, Vishnu, Shiva, Parvati, Karttikeya, Kaam, Dattatreya, Ganesh, Ram, Gauri Gayatri, Lakshmi, Sarasvati, and other deities). Many are dedicated to smaller deities (Nag Panchami, Hanuman Jayanti, cows, rivers – Jamna and Ganges, hills, lakes, one's guru, rishi, spirits, plants, chariots (Ratha Saptami), small pox etc.

Certain days are auspicious – if a full moon falls on a Thursday it is regarded as auspicious for charitable acts. A festival may be observed with acts of worship, fasting, bathing, fairs (Kumbh Mela), recitation of sacred hymns (Mantras), lighting lamps (Diwali), or feeding and offering gifts to Brahmins.

It is impossible to give a complete list of fasts and festivals as they vary from place to place and community to community. The important festivals and fasts are mentioned in this book. All the fasts and festivals are arranged alphabetically.

Ceremonies

The social structure of the Hindus represents a unique system of its own, the principles of which are not found in the same measure anywhere else in the world. The Hindu ceremonies are expressive; contain symbolic performances, dramatic utterances and theological gestures. They give expression to aspirations and ideals of the Hindus. The main aim of the ceremonies is to secure the welfare and development of the personality of the recipient. Local customs, beliefs, traditions and manners are the sources of Hindu Dharma, ceremonies, rites and rituals. In this book only those ceremonies are mentioned which are performed in various stages of the life of an individual from conception to cremation.

The Vedas (10,000 BC) are recognized as the primary source of Dharma (righteous act or good code of conduct), traditions and practices of the Hindus. After the Vedas, Brahmanas are source of ceremonies, rituals and rites of Hindus. They also explain the purpose and meaning of the sacraments. Upnishads are mainly concerned with philosophical subjects, but they also contain references about childhood, students at the house of the guru, usefulness of the sacred Gayatri Mantra, acceptance of late marriages, unmarried pregnancy as sinful, contains many references to the naming system, and also describe hymns about cremation etc.

The first systematic treatment of the Vedic sacraments and domestic ceremonies are found in the Sutra literature (6 BC). The Grihasutras mentions all the ceremonies, rites, rituals and customs essential for a Hindu householder. These are the main sources of the ceremonies performed from pregnancy to cremation. The Dharmasutras (right, duty, law, religious custom and usage) deal with castes, and different stages of life. They contain rules about thread ceremony and marriage.

The Smritis (which is remembered) mention thread ceremony, marriage ceremony, and the worship of some deities at some occasions in life. The Puranas deal with ceremonies, customs and usages and fasts and feasts of the Hindus. Astronomical considerations that played an important part in the rituals are developed in the Puranas. In olden days the marriage ceremonies of the Greeks were similar to those of the Hindus in their broad out-lines.

Local customs have been recognised as one of the sources of Hindu ceremonies and rituals. That is why one finds a difference in marriage and birth ceremonies according to the taste and refinement of the local people concerned. But hymns at marriage and birth ceremonies are the same with slight variations in performing rites. Apart from some important and essential aspects of Hinduism, rituals from birth to cremation and Shradh ceremonies are included in this book.

Religious ceremonies are communicated to ladies by the parents and priests without reserve. I therefore requested my wife to be a partner in this book and help me in collecting materials and I am thankful to her for valuable help. We also thank the publisher for giving us an opportunity to publish the results of our research.

Ramesh Chander Dogra MBE
Urmila Dogra

1.

Fasts and Festivals

Fasts and Festivals

Hinduism is a very wide subject and so are their fasts and festivals. Only an encyclopedia of Hindu fasts and festivals can cover these themes. The Hindus are bound to keep frequent fasts through the whole year. Age, infirmity, and diseases, in extreme cases, afford exemption from this duty.

However an attempt has been made to list the important ones. Observing fasts and performing ceremonies was and is a part of Hindu way of life - leading to emancipation. Simple food, high thinking, listening to religious stories and making these teachings a part of life was considered a goal of life. The stories connected with fasts have consoled fasting Hindus as each story present some thought provoking ideas and high moral values. Each day of the week brings a special message and stories connected with fasts have consoled millions of people. In this book the authors have explained the significance and philosophy of important fasts.

Some festivals especially reserved for married women are Karva Chauth, Vata Savitri, Haritalika Teej, Teej and Gangaur. All the fasts and festivals are arranged alphabetically.

Ahoi Ashthmi

Mothers keep fast on the eighth day of the waning moon in the month of Kartik (October-November). Some mothers keep fast on this day for the welfare of their children and to maintain good relationship between mothers-in-laws and daughters-in-law.

Once upon a time there was a mother-in-law who sent her daughter-in-law to fetch some soft earth to clean their house on Ahoi Ashthmi. The daughter-in-law dug some soft earth, but unfortunately she killed some children of a porcupine who had made a hole in there. The mother of porcupine was sad to see her children dead and cursed the lady that she will remain barren in her life. When the mother-in-law heard about the curse she asked her to leave the house — as a woman without children was considered by some women as is a curse for the family. She made a small hut in the jungle and started living there with her husband. She saw a cow that was sick. She looked after the cow and when the cow got better she found out the curse of porcupine on the lady. The cow went to the porcupine and asked her to take back the curse. She agreed to take the curse back and blessed the lady for a child. She was living happily with her husband and gave birth to a child. The mother-in-law came to know about her grand child and visited them and felt sorry about her bad behaviour. She prayed that misfortunes to remain away and fortunes come to them every day, and started keeping the fast to maintain good relationship between mother-in-law and daughter-in-law.

Akha Teej (fast) ki Katha

It falls on the third day of the bright half of Vaisakh (April-May). Parshu Ram, the sixth incarnation of Vishnu was also born on this day. It is believed that a secret donation on this day can make the person and his family very prosperous in this world and also in the next life. People fast on this day and offer prayers to god on behalf of their ancestors.

The story of the fast is that the king Yudhishtra (eldest brother of Pandus) performed Rajsuya Yajna (Ygya) to pronounce that he was a king of the world. He invited many Chiefs and kings and made announcement of his donations. He was told that he was wrong in making announcement of his donations and advised that secret donations would benefit him more in this life and also in the next world. After that the king felt ashamed and decided to give secret donations and fast on Akha Teej day to get eternal salvation.

Anant Chaturdashi Vrat (fast)

This fast is related to the fourteenth day of Bhadrapada (August-September). Some women wear red garments to worship the endless god (Anant). Devotees keep fast on this day and eat food without salt. The people tie Anant (a sacred thread with fourteen knots) on their arms. Women tie on their left arm and men tie it on their right arm. They consider the sacred thread is Lord Vishnu and its incarnations, which gives victory in life and emancipation from seven deadly sins (pride, covetousness, lust, anger, gluttony, envy and sloth).

Dharma the eldest of Pandavas, asked Krishna to tell him of a fast (Vrat), which would grant him a kingdom along with prosperity for life. Krishna said that a Brahman named Sumantu married Diksha, the charming daughter of Bhrigu Rishi. Diksha died after giving birth to a daughter called Sheela.

Sumantu married another woman called Karkasha. She was irritable, quarrelsome and troublesome. Sheela was very beautiful and got married to saint Kaudinya. Sumantu was not hospitable to Kaudinya (son-in-law). Kaudinya and Sheela left and started their journey to their home. On the way they found a large number of woman in red garments, on the bank of a river, worshipping the endless god Anant, on the 14th day of Bhadrapad. The newly married Sheela also performed puja as told by these women. Due to the worship she and her husband became rich and prosperous. One day her husband saw the fourteen knotted thread on her arm and got annoyed, snatched the thread and threw it in fire. Sheela saved a bit of the thread from the fire and put it in a pot full of milk. Kaudinya lost all his wealth due to the insult he gave to Anant (thread). Sheela told her husband that they were going through bad times because of the insult he had given to Anant. He repented and prayed unto the endless god Anant for forgiveness. He went to the forest to find Anant. He sat down under a mango tree full of vermin of all sorts. He asked the tree whether he had seen Lord Anant. The tree replied, Oh Brahman – I have not seen him. He went further and met (i) cow and her calf, (ii) two lakes full of lotuses, lilies etc, (iii) donkey and an elephant, and asked all of them whether they had seen Lord Anant. All of them replied that they had not seen the Lord Anant. Kaudinya got very tired of his stupidity and prayed to god to guide him. At that moment Anant appeared before Kaudinya as an old Brahman and took him to a cave to have a glimpse of the Lord. He saw the Lord and asked forgiveness of breaking the sacred thread. The Lord told him to observe the Anant's fast for fourteen years to get rid of the sin of breaking the Anant (thread) and throwing it in fire. He also explained that the mango tree under which you sat was a learned scholar of Vedas in his previous life, but he did not impart knowledge to his students. The vermins on the tree were his pupils. The cow was a land, which swallowed the seed and did not give crops to its farmer. Her calf was justice who could not identify between real and false. The lakes were two sisters and they exchanged gifts between themselves but did not give anything in donation. The donkey was anger and elephant was egotism. The old Brahman was Anant himself and cave was the world.

The Lord disappeared and Kaudinya came to his home and observed fast for fourteen years and became prosperous and lived a happy life with his wife and children.

Anvala Sinchini Ekadshi Vrat

This Vrat is observed on the eleventh day of the bright half of Phalgun (February-March) and usually the following story is told before breaking the fast.

Once there was a pious lady living in a remote village with her son and daughter-in-law. She was well known in the surrounding villages for charitable work and donations to the needy people. She used to keep this fast every year and donate a golden Anvali to some temple or a poor person. Anvala is one of the species of plums from Indian mountains. For her devotion to god and also to the Anvala Sinchini Ekadshi Vrat (fast) she was awarded by god the reward of perpetual happiness and prosperity in her family life. Whenever a needy person from a neighbouring village needed some help, she would willingly help the person. She was also helpful and merciful to her own village people.

Her son and his wife resented her charity work and told her to stop giving away so much gold and money to village people. She believed that god has given her plenty of wealth and she must share some part of it with poor people. Her son and his wife disagreed and wanted her to stop the donation work immediately. She did not agree with her son and left all her wealth to her son and his wife and told them that she was going to live in a hut in a nearby jungle.

In the jungle on Ekadshi day she kept fast and did not have any money to give in charity. She made clay Anvala and donated it to a nearby temple. She was always ready to help the needy people. Soon she became very popular in the surrounding villages. On the next Ekadshi day she kept fast and made another clay Anvala and donated it to a temple in the next village to her hut. After worshipping in the temple she was walking back to her hut when she heard a divine echo that she was a pious lady and god has changed her hut into a beautiful house with all the good things and food she needs for herself and for her charity work. On reaching near her hut she was surprised that her hut has become a beautiful house and everything required for charity work is inside the house. The lady again started sharing her wealth with the poor and needy people. She became very popular in the surrounding villages for her acts of charity. She also started giving free food every day to the poor people in the temple near to her house.

In the meantime her son and his wife became very poor, as the god has cursed them for not allowing the pious lady to continue her charity work. The son and daughter-in-law of the lady heard about free food given to poor people in a temple in the next village. They went there and ate to their fill. Next day again they went to the temple to eat food and her son recognized his mother and apologized and begged her pardon. The pious lady felt sad about the sad condition of her son and his wife. She assured them good life if they promise to keep fast and help the poor in need. She asked them to keep the fast and pray to god for inner spiritual strength to obtain success in all undertakings. She returned with them to her original house and they all became happy and prosperous.

Baisakhi

The name is derived from the Vikrami month Vaisakh. The Baisakhi festival falls on or about 13th April. In the Panjab it marks the ripening of the rabi harvest, the happy time for the peasant as he gathers the fruit of his labour. In some parts of the State it is considered a good omen to apply sickle to the crop for the first time on this day. The farmers go to fairs and perform the Bhangra dance. The dancers and the drummers challenge each other to continue the dance, and the scenes of sowing, harvesting, winnowing and gathering of crop are expressed by zestful movements of the body, to the accompaniment of ballads. The Baisakhi has a special significance for the Sikhs. It was on Baisakhi day in AD 1699 that the tenth Guru, Guru Gobind Singh, founded the order of the Khalsa. The Sikhs were converted into a martial community by instituting the custom of Pahul (baptism).

The Arya Samaj celebrates the Baisakhi day, as it was on this day in 1875 that Swami Daya Nand set up the first Arya Samaj in Bombay.

On this day Hindus and Sikhs visit temples or Gurdwaras to pay their obeisance. Fairs are held in various parts of the Panjab. Baisakhi fair at Damdama Sahib in Bhhatinda - a fair at Damdama Sahib is being held annually for three days for the last 300 years. After the fierce battles of Anandpur, Chamkur and Muktsar against the Mughals, Guru Gobind Singh retired to the jungles of Malwa. Talwandi Sabi where he took rest (dam) is known as Damdama Sahib. The Guru stayed there for nine months in 1705. It is the headquarters of the Nihangs, a warrior sect among the Sikhs, founded by Akali Phula Singh. There are ten Gurdwaras and three tanks at Damdama Sahib.

Baisakhi fair celebrated at Pindori Mahantan (Gurdaspur) is very famous. It is an old Dera (monastery) of Mahants. The fair continues for three days and is attended by a large number of people, and has an interesting programme of folk song, dance and competitions. Bhangra parties provide maximum entertainment and draw big crowds. They perform in the compound near the temple after paying obeisance to the Mahant and getting his blessings. The leading singer recites loudly a small couplet at the end of which the players start dancing. In every party there is a clown who dances in competition with a lady (man in female clothes). The dancers jerk and twist their arms and bodies with remarkable agility.

Some people claim that the sacred river Ganges came from heaven to earth on Baisakhi day, and on this day people go to have a bath in the holy river. It is believed that whosoever takes bath with full devotion in Ganges attains salvation.

Bhagvad-Gita *see* **Gita Jayanti**

Bhaiya dooj or Bhau Bij or Bhaiduj or Bhratridwitya

The festival is observed on the second day of Kartik (October-November), and is dedicated for the welfare of brothers. Brothers visit their sisters on this day and sisters appease them by offering them sweets, praying for their long and happy family life. It is said that Yamuna often asked her brother Yama (god of death) to visit her house and dine, but he evaded. At last, moved by repeated invitations, he went on this day to his sister's house and was sumptuously treated.

He was pleased and asked her for a blessing. She said, that he should come to her house on this day every year and should grant happiness to all those brothers who visit their sister's on this day. He granted this request and that is why all brothers are well treated, and they live happily throughout the year.

There is another story regarding this festival. Once there was an old lady who had seven daughters-in-law. All the daughters-in-law had brothers except the younger one. She was crying, as she had no brother to visit her on Bhaiya dooj day. She was surprised to see a man visiting her as her brother. She offered her brother food and sweets and in return he gave her a present of pebbles and leaves. She did not want to show the present to her other six sinter-in-laws, but after a great compulsion, she took them to a room where she has kept the pebbles. She never knew that the pebbles and leaves had turned into precious stones and costly clothes. Every body thought that the brother was a god in form of an ordinary person.

In this festival a sister takes her seat in front of her brother, and after lighting the lamp she marks the forehead of her brother with white sandal paste three times. She does it with the little finger of her left hand; sometimes some other female member of the family may blow the conch-shell. She also prays to god for the long, healthy, happy and prosperous life of her brother. In return brother also prays to god for her long and happy life and gives her some gift in cash or kind. In the end the sister offers a feast in honour of her brother. The theme of the festival is love, affection and respect for each other.

Bhisham Panchak Vvrat (fast)

Bhishama the most noble and upright of all heroes of the Mahabharata, was the son of king Shantanu (of Hastinapur) and the river goddess Ganga. He was a devoted son and always kept his words. On the 11th of Kartik (October-November), General Bhishma of Kaurva's army was laid on his deathbed on the battlefield, but he had the power of fixing the time of his death, he lived till the sun had crossed the vernal equinox. During the period he lay on the bed of arrows erected by Arjuna, he was advising the Pandavas, how to rule justly and fairly, and how to attain heaven in the end. Therefore some people fast on these days and spend their time in reading his advice and Mahabharata.

Budhvaar (Wednesday) ki Katha

All those who keep fast on Wednesday (Planet Mercury) take their meals once a day in the afternoon. The use of green articles is associated with this fast. Usually the fast is also observed in the honor of Lord Shiva. The fast promotes happiness and prosperity to husband, wife and their children. Wednesday is also connected with the Planet Mercury.

Once a couple lived happily. The wife went to her parents for holidays. After some time the husband went to his father-in-law's house to bring his wife. He went on Sunday and spent Sunday, Monday, and Tuesday in hospitality and wanted to bring his wife back home on Wednesday. He was told that it was inauspicious to start a journey on Wednesday, as planet Mercury is not in favour of daughters leaving their parental home on Wednesday. The Son-in-law did not agree and started journey to his home on Wednesday. On the way his wife felt thirsty and he went to get some water. In the meantime Lord Mercury disguised as her husband brought some water to quench her thirst. Within a short time her husband came and was surprised to see a man of his resemblance sitting next to his wife. The matter went to the king to find out who was the real husband. In the evening they were put in different cells. In the morning one cell was empty. The king said that the missing person was Mercury. The Mercury rules on Wednesday and the husband challenged him to start his journey on Wednesday. The Mercury got offended and disguised as her husband to teach a lesson to the real husband. The real husband and wife got together and started their journey to their home and told the story to their family members and friends.

Chaitra Gauri

Gauri (yellow or brilliant) is a name of the wife of Lord Shiva. She is worshipped in the month of Chaitra (March-April) by every married women, whose husband is alive, and unmarried women, On the third of the month a brass swing containing images of Shiva and family are placed on a raised dais, and the images are worshipped every morning. A fresh wreath of flowers has to be added every day. The ladies meet on selected days in a house and worship the image of Gauri, after dressing her with beautiful clothes and ornaments. Fruits, sweets and flowers are freely distributed to all visitors. There are generally many invitations on one day and many women are seen going from house to house in the best of spirits. The gathering is called Halad-Kanku (turmeric and saffron) ceremony.

Chitra Purnima

Chitra Purnuma falls on the full moon day of Chaitra (March-April) during the ascendancy of Chitra star. The star is particularly sacred to Chitrgupta, a record keeper in the abodes of the dead, who records the virtues and vices of humans.. He is the recorder of Yama (god of death). A Havan (fire worship) is performed, and prayers are offered to Chitragupt on Chitra Purnima day. Some sweets are prepared and distributed as Prasad or holy sacrament. The worship of Chitragupt reminds us to keep on doing good things in life because on the judgment day Chitragupt will read out the balance-sheet of each person's deeds, which are recorded in his great register (Agra Sandhani). The good and evil deeds are reckoned and judgment passed by Yama. The good people are then sent to one of the higher abode or worlds, and the sinful are sent to hell. The festival Chitra Purnima, on the full-moon day of the month of Chaitra is dedicated to Chitragupta. The following is a story connected with this festival.

Brihaspati (a Rishi and also regent of the planet Jupiter) is the Guru or teacher of Indra, and is the suppliant, the priest, who intercedes with gods on behalf of men and protects mankind against the wicked. During the absence of the Guru, Indra did many bad things. When the Guru came back Indra repented and asked him what he should do to get rid of the sins he had committed during his absence.

Brihaspati sent him on a pilgrimage to South India. At Madurai he discovered a Shiv Ling and built a temple at that place and started worshipping the Linga. Soon god blessed him and his sins were removed as well. The day on which he worshipped the Lingam was Chitra Purnima day. It is believed that if you worship god with devotion on Chitra Purnima day and obey your Guru sincerely, your sins will be washed away. On this day people worship god with Kalsa (vessel filled with water) to get rid of their sins. People feed the poor and needy and give money in charity on Chitra Purnima day.

Dattatreya Jayanti

The birthday (jayanti) of Dattatreya falls on the full moon day of Magh (January-February). People fast and pray throughout the day, listen to the teachings of Dattatreya and make a resolve that they will follow his teachings. The story of the saint Dattareya is as follows:

He was the son of Maharishi Atri and Ansuya (lady of perfect virtue). She performed severe austerities for a long time until trinity (Brahma, Vishnu and Mahesh) came to her in the form of Sanyasins (ascetics). They asked the chaste lady what she would like to have and she replied: three sons like Brahma, Vishnu and Mahesh (Shiva).

The three gods fulfilled her wish there by becoming three boy babies. Suddenly Ansuya felt milk flowing into her breasts. When her husband arrived she did not have to explain anything since he knew everything already. He embraced his three sons together and they became one child with two feet, three heads and six arms. The three gods told sage Atri that your three-headed child would grow up to become a great sage who would possess the combined knowledge and power of the three gods (Brahma, Vishnu and Mahesh). Dattatreya was soon worshipped by many sages and taught the Vedanta doctrine of self-realization. He was a person of gentle, peaceful and loving character. His birthday is celebrated every year.

One day, Dattatreya was asked why he was so happy and cheerful. Here is a part of his reply:

> The earth taught me patience and generosity.
> The ocean taught me to remain the same inspire of storms.
> The fire taught me to give myself so that I would shine brightly.
> The air taught me to move freely and not stay in one place.
> The water taught me how much purity is needed for good health.
> The sky taught me to be above everything and yet embrace all things.
> The moon taught me that the self remains the same even when the appearance changes.
> The sun taught me that a luminous face is reflected by all smooth surfaces
> The dove taught me that love means feeding one's family.
> The bee taught me to collect sweet wisdom from places where no one suspected it to be.
> The arrow-maker taught me to be purposeful and always concentrate on one point.
> The snake taught me to be content to live in a hole or cave and build no house.
> The fish taught me never to take the bait and so destroy myself.
> The owl taught me to sit peacefully and be content with little food.
> The deer taught me never listen to lewd songs.

Dattatreya learnt wisdom from whatever source it came.

Devachi Chauth

This is the fourth day of the first half of the month of Shravan (July-August). It is sacred to Ganesh and his mother

Gauri. Yellow and red silk threads are taken. Sixteen knots are given to the red thread and twenty-one knots are given to the yellow thread. Each such thread is then worshipped. The yellow ones represent Gauri and the red ones represent Ganesh. The number of the amulets thus prepared corresponds with the number of girls and boys in the family. Sweets are prepared and a feast takes place. The red silk amulets are tied to the arms of the boys and the yellow ones to the arms of the girls. Sweets are distributed to all present in the house. It is believed that amulets bring good luck and prosperity to the bearer.

Dhan Teras ki Katha

It is Dhantrayodashi, the thirteenth day of the waxing moon in the month of Ashwin (September-October) i.e. two days before the Diwali day. People clean their houses and invite Lakshmi (Goddess of wealth) by lighting an earthen lamp at the doorstep of their houses. Once Lord Vishnu and his wife Lakshmi visited the planet earth and stayed under a Peepal tree. Lord Vishnu went away on an urgent visit and told her not to look towards south until he return, Unfortunately she could not resist looking towards the south as it was full of beautiful flowers and sugarcane-fields. As a punishment for not obeying the Lord she was asked to work in a farmer's field for twelve years. After twelve years Lakshmi wanted to be free and the farmer told her that due to her company his family has become very happy and prosperous and would not like her to leave his house. The farmer saw a dream that goddess Lakshmi was in their house and that is why they were becoming prosperous and rich. The goddess was impressed by their devotion towards her and told them that tomorrow is Dhan Teras therefore you clean your house and light the earthen lamp at the door and you can worship me, but I will remain invisible in your house. The farmer did as he was told and became very rich and prosperous. People still believe the story and worship the goddess for happiness and wealth. Some people also keep fast on this day.

Diwali/Deepavali (row of lights) or the festival of lamps (lights)

Diwali means a row of lights. It is observed on the last two days of the dark fortnight of the month of October-November, and is celebrated by the Hindus all over India or abroad. In Bengal the festival is dedicated to the worship of Kali. In South India some people take an oil bath in the morning and new clothes are worn. People distribute sweet meats. They light fireworks, which are regarded as the effigies of Narakasura, the wicked giant, who was killed on this day by Lord Krishna.

Everyone is happy to forgive and forget the wrongs done by others. The festival is a great unifying force. Every one buy new clothes, worship goddess Lakshmi and give a lot of things in charity to the poor and needy. People clean their houses during day and illuminate their houses at night with earthen oil-lamps.

To some the festival signifies the victory of justice, dharma, and ahimsa over injustice, adharma, and violence. The festival also commemorates the birth of Lakshmi, wife of Vishnu, goddess of wealth and fortune. Some believe that illumination of lamps on this day is to celebrate Lord Rama's victory over Ravana.

It lasts for five days in some communities. In general the first day of Diwali/Divali is dedicated to the goddess Lakshmi and Parvati, and windows are kept open to welcome them into the homes. The business class (Baniyas), close their accounts on this day. They make piles of coins on their ledgers and top the money with an image of Lakshmi, and worship her as the giver of wealth. Some people, especially business communities, spend the second day in gambling, especially with dice. In villages women also draw colourful geometrical designs known as Rangoli on the floor near thresholds and in the courtyards of their houses.

On this day goddess Lakshmi is worshipped in the evening after all day fast. The third day commemorates the victory of Vishnu over the demon king Bali, and on this day Lakshmi Puja is also undertaken. At the end the family dinner is served and the fast comes to an end, and the goddess is worshipped in the evening after an all day fast. In Bengal the goddess Kali is the object of worship. The fourth and last day is Diwali proper, when little earthen bowls filled with oil are lighted and placed in rows inside and outside the house. This is called the return of Rama to Ayudhiya and his coronation. The business communities keep it as the first day of the year of Vikram era. It is the day when King Vikramaditya ascended the throne and is celebrated by them as the New Year.

Amongst Sikhs Diwali is also celebrated with great pomp and show. On Diwali day Bhai Buddha, the first Granthi (priest), completed his perusal of the Granth and it consequently became a Sikh holiday. The day is celebrated with a great fair held at the Golden Temple (Amritsar), which is attended, by Sikhs and Hindus. The celebration of Diwali extends over three days at the Golden Temple. Starting a day earlier than the general Diwali, the celebrationas reach a peak on the night of Diwali, when the temple is elegantly illuminated and the most gorgeous fire works with enhanced effects, because of the reflection in the tank, thrill the mammoth gathering. It is stated that in the middle of the seventeenth century, Jahangir (Emperor of India) arrested 52 Rajas and Guru Hargovind (sixth Guru). He felt uncomfortable and released 52 Rajas along with the Guru - who reached Amritsar on the eve of Diwali. The people illuminated the temple and the city to celebrate his return. On Diwali religious gatherings are held at Maji Sahib, Akal Takht and Baba Atal, which continue for three days. On Diwali people visit Gurdwaras to pay their obeisance.

Durga Puja

The festival is observed twice a year, in the month of Chaitra (March-April) and in Aswin (September-October). On the first of Chaitra (March-April) begins the celebration of the birth of Lord Ram (seventh incarnation of Vishnu). Every evening sermons are delivered by professional priests in all temples dedicated to Ram until the ninth day, when as soon as the sun reaches the meridian, the birth is celebrated with great éclat. In the sermons prominence is given to stories from the Ramayana.

Durga Puja is celebrated in Aswin (September-October) and it lasts for nine days, in honour of nine manifestations of Durga. The word Nava-ratri means nine nights. It is a great Hindu feast celebrating Durga. Devotees observe fast and pray to the goddess for heath and prosperity. Durga Puja is offered in various parts of India to propitiate the goddess for mercy, protection, wealth, health and prosperity.

Durga or Devi the goddess is the wife of Lord Shiva and daughter of Himvat. She is mentioned in Mahabharata under a variety of names. As a Shakti (female energy of Shiva) she has two characters, one mild, the other fierce; and it is under the latter that she is especially worshipped. She has a variety of names - referring to her various forms and actions.

In her milder form she is Uma (light and a type of beauty), Gauri (yellow or brilliant), Parvati (mountaineer and Himavati from her parentage), Jagat-mata (mother of the world) and Bhavani.

In her terrible form she is Durga (the inaccessible), Kali (the black), Chandi (the fierce), and Bhairvi (the terrible). It is in this character the bloody sacrifices are offered to her during Durga Puja. She has ten arms and in most of her hands she has weapons. As Kali or Kalika (black), she is represented with a black skin, face dripping with blood, encircled with snakes, hung round with skull and heads of demons. As Vindhya-vasini (dweller in Vindhyas), she is worshipped at Mirzapur where Vindhyas approach the

Ganges. As a Durga she rides on a tiger in a fierce and menacing attitude. She is renowned slayer of demons, and is actually supposed to be goddess Kali. She killed Mahisha (buffalo demon), demons Sumbha and Nisumbha. She also killed demon Raktavija (blood sprinkling demon – as each drop of his blood had the power to become a demon), and Tripurasura.

During Durga Puja devotees will make clay images of the goddess, which they will worship for nine days, and after that it will be immersed in the water. During the nine days devotees either fast or take only one meal. If they are unable to do so, they observe the fast for seven days, five or three days, at least. A special ritualistic worship of the mother is conducted daily from Durga Sapashati. On Vijay Dashami (10th day) nine girls below the age of ten are worshipped as the embodiment of divine mother. On this day a Havan (Yajana) is performed in the temple with recitation from Durga Saptashati in praise of mother goddess. The recitation of mantras (hymns) and worship is performed in the right royal fashion. Brahmans and poor people are fed, and cash and clothes are given in charity.

The origin of the Navaratri is thus given. When Rama found that as soon as he cut off any heads of Ravan, they came to life again. All the gods became alarmed at this phenomenon and prayed to goddess Devi. She awoke at midnight of the first day of Ashwin (September-October) and blessed Rama – that he would be able to kill Ravana. The gods were grateful and decided to fast and worship the goddess. They performed Puja in the best possible way and Rame killed Ravana on the eighth day. The goddess appeared before the gods and they ignited the sacred fire on the ninth day and offered sacrifices. On the tenth day Rama started back triumphantly for his capital and therefore this day is called Vijay Ḍashami or Dussehra (Vijay means success and Dashami means the tenth day).

Lord Shiva permitted his wife Parvati, daughter of Himavant (Himalayas) to go and see her mother only during these nine days once a year, after which her mother had to send her back. The women make images to which they attach themselves like a mother to her daughter, whom she has to let go to her husband. Devotees make this festival into a series of spiritual exercises in which they confess their sins to the goddess, and then ask her help in their enterprises. In Bengal members of family who live away from home return during the festival and stay together.

Dussehra

Dussehra is observed during the first half of the month Ashvin (September-October) and lasts for ten days. The tenth day is called Vijayadasami (the victorious tenth day). This festival lasts ten days. It is celebrated all over India, and is connected with the autumn equinox. In Bengal it commemorates the victory of Durga/Kali, wife of Shiva, over a buffalo-headed demon. The image of Durga is worshipped daily until the end of the festival, when it is cast into a river. In North India the Ram Lila or events of Rama's life are enacted on the same day as the Durga Puja in Bengal. It commemorates the victory of Rama over Ravana or the victory of virtue over vice. During this festival alms are freely distributed, musicians go about playing on their instruments and demanding gifts.

A pageant is gone through consisting of an outdoor theatrical representation of the storming of Ravana's castle. In the midst of the fortress is the giant Ravana with ten heads and arms, each grasping a weapon, and bristling with fireworks, besides him sits Sita, the wife of Ram, whom the giant Ravana had abducted. Rama demands the restitution of his wife, which is refused; the besiegers then advance to attack. Conspicuous among among the assailants is Hanuman with army of men dressed as monkeys. Sita is rescued after a mock battle and Ravana's effigy is blown up, thus bringing to a close. It is a festival appreciated by every creed. The festival basically commemorates the victory of Virtue over vice.

Eclipse (Surya Grahan)

When the gods and demons churned the ocean, nectar came out of it. Vishnu assumed the form of a Mohini (charming woman), deluded the demons, and gave nectar only to the gods. Rahu assumed the shape of a god and started drinking nectar. The Sun and the Moon saw him, and reported it to Vishnu, for only the gods may drink the nectar of immortality. Vishnu took his disc and cut the monster's neck. The head of the monster Rahu stayed in the sky alive and his body (called Ketu) fell on earth. In revenge to this betrayal Rahu and Ketu periodically eclipse the sun and the moon. Astronomically speaking, when the sun, the moon and the earth are all in a line, with the moon or earth at the center, a lunar eclipse takes place respectively.

Devotees who worship the almighty at the time of the eclipse drive great benefits. At the time of eclipse people bathe in the sacred rivers. People give a lot of things in charity and feed the poor and needy after the eclipse. After the eclipse they clean their houses and, vessels, etc., and take a bath before they start cooking. Some people also observe a fast during the eclipse.

Ekaadshi ki Katha

The eleventh day of Kartik (October-November) is called Prabodhini Ekaadhshi. It is considered especially meritorious to fast on this day because Lord Vishnu who had gone to sleep on the 10th of Ashaadh (June-July) awoke on this day at the request of his wife. Lord Vishnu's wife Lakshmi was very unhappy about his long sleep. He promised to reduce his sleep to four months. Lakshmi was happy about it and announced that she would visit those houses where religious assemblies would be held on this day. Since that time people observe fast on this day with great devotion.

Baths in the morning, visits to temples, gifts to poor people and prayers to Lord Vishnu are all advised. In Kartik Mahatmya it is mentioned that a Brahman named Dev Sharma married his daughter Gunavati to one of his pupil called Chandra. One day a demon killed Chandra and Gunavati became a widow, but she kept on keeping Ekaadshi fast. She used to go to the Ganges for her bath. Lord Vishnu was very much impressed by her devotion. The Lord came down in his celestial car and took her to heaven

Later she became Lord Krishna's (eighth incarnation of Vishnu) wife as Satyabhama, and her father was reborn as Satrajit and her husband as Akrur. Akrur was an uncle of Lord Krishna and Satrajit was the son of Nigha who got Syamantaka gem for his devotion to the Sun god. The eleventh day (Ekaadshi) is therefore regarded as very efficacious fast day for securing happiness in future.

There is another story, which says that people will get rid of all their sins if they keep this, fast in full faith, and those who keep this fast half-heartedly will not get full benefit. Once there was a king who was a very religious man. His entire subject kept the Ekaadshui fast regularly. He married his daughter to a prince who kept the fast half-heartedly, and therefore during the night the prince got sick and died. As he had kept the fast, he had earned the blessings of gods for securing happiness in future. In his next birth the prince became a very powerful king. One day a Brahman from the princess's kingdom visited the new king and recognized him as the prince who died. The Brahman told the story to the princess and led her to the king. She was surprised to find him with the blessings of god. He welcomed his wife and made her sit next to her on the throne. The husband and wife were united again due to the fast and lived a very happy life with their children.

Ganesh Chaturthi also known as Siddhi Vinayak Chaturthi

Ganesh - an elephant headed is the god of wisdom and remover of obstacles: hence he is invariably propitiated at the beginning of any important undertaking, and is invoked at the commencement of books. He wrote Mahabharata from the dictation of Vyas and is the son of Shiva and Parvati. Each part of his physical form conveys a message: the elephant head conveys knowledge by listening through the ears; the tusks symbolize perfection and imperfection in this world. The trunk stands for physical and mental strength; the large stomach depicts the ability to digest whatever experience life brings; the rat (his vehicle) stands for desire, wealth and removal of obstacles. He has four hands: in one hand he holds an axe and a goad – the axe is to remove obstacles and the goad is to keep his devotees on the path of dharma (righteousness). The snare in the other hand symbolises his control over death. In his bottom left hand he holds a sweetmeat, representing a reward for devotion; and with his lower right hand he blesses his devotees.

Lord Ganesh grants Siddhi (success) and that is why he is also called Siddhi Vinayak (Ganesh). Ganesh gives and Ganesh takes, and therefore Ganesh is the salvation of both. When breaking the fast the worshipper should first offer food to a Brahman and give something in charity and then eat nothing cooked with or fried in oil. It is believed that he who worships Siddhi Vinayak gets what he wants i.e., knowledge, wealth and success etc. Ganesh should be worshipped first before praying to other gods or goddesses.

Ganesh Chaturthi is one of the most popular of Hindu fasts and festivals. This is the birthday of Lord Ganesh. It falls on the fourth day of the bright fortnight of Bhadrapada (August September). On this day Hindus observe fast to celebrate the birthday of Lord Ganesh. People get up early on this day, take bath, worship the idol of Ganesh and keep a fast. At the end of the festival the clay idol is thrown into the water and left to sink. Ganesha Chaturthi is especially popular in western and central India and Rajasthan.

People do not look at the moon on this day as it behaved badly towards the Ganesha because the former once laughed at him when he fell off his rat. The moon thereupon craved pardon for having disturbed the equanimity of the son of Shiva; but the curse was only removed on condition that, before looking upon the moon, everybody should hear the story of "Samantakam".

On the advice of Narad Muni Lord Krishna observed this fast to get rid of the stigma of stealing the diamond (Syamantaka Mani). Satrajit, son of Nighaa got as a gift the wonderful Syamantaka gem from the Sun god for his devotion to the god. He gave the gem to his brother, who was eaten by a lion, and Jambuwant killed the lion in order to get the gem. Without knowing the fact Satrajit blamed Krishna for taking the gem.

Krishna realised that Jambuwant had taken the gem. He had a fight with Jambuwant and defeated him. The gem was recovered and restored to Satrajit by Krishna. Satrajit was ashamed for blaming Krishna for taking the gem. In return he presented his daughter Satyabhama in marriage to Krishna.

Why it is forbidden to look at the moon on the fast day. Moon insulted Lord Ganesh and he cursed the moon on that day. Therefore any one who sees moon on that day get the curse. To get rid of the curse, keep fast on every fourth day of the bright half of the lunar month. Pray, make offering to Ganesh according to your status and also give something in charity to be free from the sin of seeing the moon.

Pray sincerely to Lord Ganesh and he will remove your difficulties in life and make your family happy and prosperous.

Ganga Snaan (Bath in river Ganges)

The sacred river Ganges is mentioned in Vedas twice and in Puranas it is known as heavenly Ganges. The Puranas represent the Viyad-Ganga, or heavenly Ganges, to flow from the toe of Vishnu, and to have been brought down from heaven, by the prayers of the saint Bhagirath, to purify the ashes of the sixty thousand sons of king Sagara, who had been burnt by the angry glance of the sage Kapila. Ganga was angry at being brought down from heaven, and Lord Shiva, to save the earth from the shock of her fall, caught the river on his brow, and checked its course with his matted locks. From this action Shiva is called Ganga-dhara (upholder of the Ganges).

Ganges snaan (bath) falls on the full moon day of Kartik (October-November). Some people observe fast on this day and sing songs in praise of Ganges. It is believed that whosoever takes bath with full devotion in Ganges attains salvation. Once Lord Shiva told Parvati that very few people go to have a dip in Ganges with full devotion. If they do then they will be rewarded with happiness and prosperity. To prove his point Lord Shiva came to the planet earth and changed himself to a leper and Parvati as a dutiful wife dressed in simple clothes. They both sat near the Ganges and Parvati requested many people, but no one agreed to help her in carrying her leper husband for a dip in the Ganges. After a long wait one person took pity on Parvati and stopped to pick up the leper for a dip in the Ganges. He thought that helping the helpless people is as good as a dip in the Ganges and presumed that the leper might get cured of the disease after a bath in the Ganges. As soon he touched the leper, Lord Shiva and Parvati came in their usual form and blessed the man. He came back to his village and told every one the story and was pleased that Lord Shiva and Parvati had blessed him for a happy and prosperous life.

Gangaur (Goddess Gauri) ki Katha

Gangaur fast is observed by women in honour of goddess Gauri, from the first day of Chaitra (14 March) for sixteen days. Married women observe fast for their happy married life and unmarried girls keep fast finding a faithful and perfect husband. Sixteen earthen idols of the goddess are prepared and worshipped with rice, flowers and grass. During fast women worship and sing songs in honor of the goddess. On the sixteenth day the idols are immersed in some river.

Once a farmer planted grass for king's horses, but he found some girls were plucking grass to offer at the worship. He was not happy but the girls assured him that no harm will come to his grass field, and the goddess will also reward him. On the last fast day the girls brought a lot of food for the farmer and his family to compensate him for the loss of grass. The farmer's wife stored the surplus food and prayed to the goddess for her family's prosperity. After some time she was surprised to find her storeroom full of gold, diamonds, pearls and ornaments. The farmer was surprised to see his field full of green grass for the king's horses. From that time onwards the farmer's wife kept the fast and the farmer joined his wife in offering prayers to the goddess.

Gayatri Mantra Japa Day

Gayatri Japa Day is observed on the day after the Raksha Bandhan (July-August). The day is a very holy and glorious day. The Gayatri Mantra is the impregnable spiritual armour that protects its votary. The Mantra is the Divine power that transforms the human into the Divine, and blesses the aspirant with the brilliant light of the highest spiritual illumination.

A most sacred verse of the Rig Veda, which it is the duty of every Hindu to repeat mentally in his morning and evening prayers. It is addressed to the sun as Savitri, the generator, and so it is called also Savitri. Personified as a goddess, Savitri is the wife of Brahma, mother of the four Vedas. It was composed in a metre, consisting of twenty-four syllables arranged as a triplet of eight syllables each. Many Vedic hymns were composed in this metre, the most sacred being the Gayatri Mantra. It consists of a short prayer or mantra as follows:

Om Bhur Bhuvah Svaha Tat Savitu Varenyam Bhargo Devasya Dhimahi Dhiyo Yo Nah Prachodyaat.

Om (means Brahma, Vishnu, Mahesh) Bhur (earth) Bhuvah (sky) Svaha (heaven) Tat (the essence) Savitu (the creator – divine light – sun) Varenyam (is worth worshipping) Bhargo Devasya Dhimahi (upon the glory we meditate) Dhiyo Yo Nah Prachodyaat (the intellect which us may guide).

It means – let us meditate on the most excellent light of the Creator (the divine Sun); may the Almighty guide our intellect and illuminate our minds.

Gayatri Mantra Japa every day will shower upon one incalculable benefits and blessings. One who desires to attain heaven should recite thousand times Gayatri Mantra; an unlimited number gives the fulfillment of all desires. The presiding deity of the Mantra is naturally the sun god. Each letter of the Mantra has its own deity who wipes away all sins from the person who repeats it. By means of it the sacrifice is carried to the gods, and hence it is said to be Agni metre.

Gita Jayanti

It is the birthday of Bhagvad Gita (song of Divine), celebrated in India and abroad on the eleventh day of the bright half of the month of Magh (December-January). The devotees fast on this day, and it is also - Ekadshi day.

It was on this day, thousands of years ago; Sanjay narrated to king Dhritarashtra the dialogue between Lord Krishna and Arjuna. It contains the message of life that appeals to all human beings. An effulgence of light as bright as a sunrise accompanied the first recital, by the Lord Krishna himself, when he showed his true self at Arjuna's insistence. The Gita is for millions of people the most sublime work of world literature, dictated by god himself so that its language has divine power. Reciting it is relieving the experience of divine proximity.

Gita or Bhagvad-Gita – the song of the Divine One. Krishna as a god, is a manifestation of Vishnu. As a man, he was related to both the Pandavas and the Kauravas, and refused to take up arms on either side, but he consented to act as a charioteer of Arjuna. When the opening hosts were drawn up in array against each other, Arjuna, touched with compunction for the approaching slaughter of kindred and friends, appeals to Krishna for guidance. Krishna teaches Arjuna the doctrine of Bhakti (faith) and to exalt the duties of a Kshatriya above all other obligations, including those of friendship and kindred. So Arjuna is told to do his duty as a soldier without heeding the slaughter of friends. Righteous conduct is more efficacious than gifts made to priests. Ancient faith in sacrifice as the sole means of liberation is no longer valid. Only Karma (deeds) and devotion to god can lead to salvation.

This is the nucleus of Hindu philosophy; everything that happens is the manifestation of immutable universal laws. The warrior must fight and kill, the victim must die, both should do so resignedly, since it is their destiny. All those things are created by me says Krishna, they are in me and yet I am distinct from them. Gita teaches faith, devotion, and pantheistic theology of the Vedanta. Krishna speaks for the protection of the good, for the destruction of the wicked and to establish righteousness. Gita has been translated into almost all the important languages of the world

Govardhan ki Katha

Govardhan festival is celebrated on the first day of the bright half of Kartik (October-November). Govardhan image is made and worshipped for wealth and prosperity. Sweets are exchanged between families and delicious food is prepared on that day to offer to Govardhan and Krishna.

People in Braj area used to worship Indra as the ruler of atmosphere and Swarg (heaven of gods). Indra had been an object of worship among the pastoral people of Braj, but Krishna persuaded them not to worship Indra, and start worshipping Govardhan Hill, because it gives you grass for your cows and also you grow food around it. Indra was greatly enraged at this, and sent a deluge of rain to overwhelm them; but Krishna lifted up the Govardhan Hill on his finger to shelter them and their cows for seven days. Indra was baffled and rendered homage to Krishna and Govardhan. Life in Braj became normal and since then people have been celebrating the festival and worshipping Govardhan Hill to keep the memory of that instance alive.

Gudhipadwa (Chaitra, March-April)

New year's day - Varsha Pratipada is the name given to the New Year day of the Shalivahan era, which is in vogue in Maharashtra. Shalivahan was the son of a potter. He became the chief of a powerful monarchy in Maharashtra. He ruled at Mungi-Paithan. The ruler whom he overthrew was Vikramaditya the last of the Gupta rulers of Malwa. Shalivahan era is reckoned from AD 78 the supposed year of his coronation. It marks the beginning of solar year. On this day Hindus raise their standard on a long pole. It is made of silk and gold clothes. Then a flower wreath is added and the whole topped by a silver or brass lota to give it the appearance of a lotus bud shaped kalash. This standard is worshipped in the usual way, and a family feast is observed. It is customary to eat a few leaves of the neem tree (Melia azadirachta) on this day, as it is supposed to prevent diseases during the year. Every one is addressed with great respect and younger members are blessed when they bow to elders.

Guru Purnima or Vyas Purnima - fast

Literally the word 'Guru' means an enlightener (Gu means darkness, Ru means light), one who provides light in darkness. Guru is a spiritual preceptor. The living guru is considered equivalent to god. Celebrated gurus sometimes receive equivalent homage in comparison to the deity. For example, the reverence in which Chaitanya Mahaprabhu is held is equivalent to that is paid to Lord Krishna.

Guru Purnima fast falls in the month of Ashad (July-August) on the full moon day in the memory of Ved Vyas, compiler of Vedas, Puranas and Mahabharata. From the imperishable nature of his works, he is called Saswat (immortal), and in his honor spiritual aspirants perform Vyas puja (worship) on this day. Disciples worship their spiritual teacher (Guru), saints, monks and men of god on this day. If the guru is present, he or she is made to sit on a chair and is worshipped like a god. In the absence of a guru, his or her idol is worshipped. People fast on this day and take food only in the afternoon after worshipping their guru.

It is believed that those who worship their guru on this day are blessed by the goddess of learning (Saraswati). The guru is the representative of god on earth and one attains salvation by worshipping and learning from the guru. Many writers present their newly published books to their guru on this day. Vyas Purnima and guru purnima is the same and is celebrated on the same day.

Amongst Sikhs - Gurparbs (fair in the memory of Gurus) are held. The most famous Gurparbs are: the birthdays of Guru Nanak and Guru Gobind Singh and the martyrdom of Guru Arjan Dev and Guru Tegh Bahadur. On Gurparbs, akhand path (non-stop recital) of Guru Granth Sahib, Kirtan and religious discourses are held in Gurdwaras.

Hanuman Jayanti

Hanuman's birthday falls on Chaitra Shukla Purnima (March-Apil) full moon day. On this day people worship Hanuman and observe fast, read Hanuman Chalisa, and worship Lord Ram. Any one who worships Lord Ram, Hanuman blesses him/her with success.

Hanuman was son of Pawan (wind) and Anjana, wife of monkey named Kesari. He was able to fly and is a conspicuous figure in the Ramayana. He and other monkeys were of divine origin, and their powers were superhuman. Hanuman jumped from India to Ceylon in one bound; he tore up trees, carried away the Himalayas, seized the clouds, and performed many other wonderful exploits. His form is as vast as mountain and as tall as gigantic tower. His complexion is yellow and glowing like molten gold. He leaps into the air and flies among the clouds with a rushing noise. In one of his fights with Ravana and the demons, they greased his tail and set it on fire, but to their surprise, he burnt down their capital city Lanka. His services to Rama were many. He acted as his spy, and fought most valiantly. He flew to the Himalayas and brought medicinal herbs to restore Lakshman to life and other wounded soldiers. After Ram's victory, he accompanied him to Ayudhya, and there he received from him the reward of perpetual life and youth. Hanuman is perfect; no one equals him in religious knowledge, in learning, and in ascertaining the sense of the scriptures. In all sciences, in the rules of austerity, he rivals the preceptor of the gods.

Haritalika Teej

Hindu women in honour of goddess Parvati observe this festival in the month of August-September. Married women and young girls keep the fast on that day in the honour of Shiva and Parvati – a renowned union in Hindu mythology and have auspicious notable features. Prayers are said so that the marriage will be as firm as Lord Shiva and goddess Parvati. The unmarried girls also keep the fast for getting a good and honest husband.

Holi

Holi is one of the major Hindu festivals, which is celebrated when the sun enters the sign of Pisces late in February. Usually the place where the Holi mound is to be set on fire is decided forty days before on Vasant Panchami, by erecting a poll there. It is a reminiscent of Maypole of Europe (pole painted and decorated with flowers for dancing around on May day in Europe). The ceremonies include the lighting of bonfires during which all evils are symbolically burnt. Women worship Holi in the afternoon. Holi fire consists of dried cow dung, and a lot of wood. It is set on fire amidst beating of drums and singing of songs in praise of Bhagat Prahlad. A burning stick is taken out and immersed in a nearby tank as a symbol of Prahlad being saved. Women keep fast on this day for the welfare of Bhagat Prahlad and collect some ash from the Holi fire to be used in the next day Gangur worship.

Some believe that Holi is a spring festival dedicated to Lord Krishna and the Gopis. It took the place of an earlier primitive fertility ritual, combining games, comic operas, suggestive songs, the throwing of coloured water, and jumping over bonfire, the ashes of which believed to possess magical powers. Some people believe that Holi is celebrated to commemorate Lord Krishna's victory over the Putana. A female demon, daughter of Bali, She attempted to kill infant Krishna by suckling him, but was herself sucked to death by the child. According to some Hindus the Holi carnival commemorates the frolics of the youthful Krishna. The festival also celebrates the death of demoness Putana, or the burning of demoness Holika sister of Hiranyakashipu, or the destruction of Kam by Shiva. Kam (god of love) inspired Shiva with amorous thoughts of Parvati while he was engaged in penitential devotion, and for his offence the god reduced him to ashes by fire from his central eye. Shiva afterwards relented him to be born again as Pradyumna (son of Krishna and Rukmani). In South India the festival ends with a midnight bonfire, in which an image of the god Kam is burned. It is not observed very much in Andhra Pradesh, though in other parts it is said to be very popular.

During the Holi festival people sprinkle each other with coloured water or even throw powder on each other or rub each other's faces with red powder. In the evening people take bath and enjoy eating and distributing sweets in the neighbourhood.

The following is the usual story told in the evening on the Holi day. Hiranyakashipu was a Daitya king who, according to Mahabharata and the Puranas, obtained from Shiva the sovereignty of three worlds for a million of years, and ordered his subject that they worship him as god. Prahlad only worshipped Vishnu as the true god and told people that a human cannot be a god. Prahlad was a pious son of a wicked father, Hiranyakashipu, the sworn enemy of Vishnu. When Prahlad insisted on worshipping Vishnu, his father ordered his death but no weapon could harm him, since Vishnu protected him.

Hiranyakashipu asked his sister Holika to kill Prahalad. She had a boon that fire can do no harm to her. She took

Prahalad in her lap and sat in a big bonfire. Holika got burnt and no harm came to Prahalad. Hiranyakashipu felt sad about his sister's death and since then people burn Holi and pray to god to protect his devotees as he protected Prahalad. Hiranyakashipu tried but could not kill his son Prahalad, but eventually he was slain by Vishnu in the Nara-Sinha (man-lion) incarnation.

Itu Worship

Itu is a name of a Bengal goddess who fulfills the wishes of her devotees. She is represented by an earthen jar filled with water and topped over by plantains.

Once upon a time a greedy Brahman from a remote village felt craving for pancakes, and asked his wife to prepare them, but the poor woman had no materials to prepare them with. The Brahman begged enough material to make the cakes. His wife started making cakes and her husband was so suspicious that he was secretly watching her all the time and tying knots to a string to record the actual number of cakes prepared. After she has made the cakes, he went to sleep. His two daughters got up early in the morning and ate one cake each. In the morning the Brahman was angry when he realized that his two girls had eaten a cake each. He took the two girls to the forest and left them there. The girls got lost in the forest and found some fairies worshipping the goddess. They also worshipped the goddess in the company of fairies and got her blessings, came back home and made their mother and father rich. Within a short time a king happened to meet the girls and married one and the other he got married to his minister. They both lived happily, but the king's wife forgot to perform the Itu worship, and the king got annoyed and divorced her. The father of the girl neglected worship and became a beggar again. He then went to his daughter who was happily married to the minister and was also performing Itu worship. The Brahman and his wife went to the girl who was performing Itu worship. On the right day she and her husband worshipped the goddess with their daughter and became rich again. The king heard a divine echo that he should bring his good wife back and ask her to perform Itu worship, and should also plant banana trees. This was done and all became prosperous and happy again and went to heaven in the end after full enjoyment of life.

Jagan-Natha (Lord of the world)

Jagan-Natha is a particular form of Krishna. He is worshipped in Bengal, Orissa and other parts of India, but Puri, near the town of Cuttack, in Orissa, is the great seat of worship, and many pilgrims visit the place from all parts of India, especially to the two great festivals of the Snana-yatra and Rath-yatra, in the month of Jyeshtha (May-June) and Ashadha (June-July). The first of these is when the image is bathed, and in the second, or car (chariot) festival, the image is brought out upon a car with the image of his brother Balram and sister Subhadra, and is drawn by the devotees. The richly decorated wooden chariot of Jagan-Nath is forty-five feet high, thirty-five feet square, with sixteen wheels each - seven feet in diameter, and is drawn by 4,200 devotees.. People visit the temple during this time and believe that they will go to heaven after death by this act of their visit to the temple. After the procession the wooden chariot is broken up and the timber is sold as relics, and a replica is made on exactly the same pattern.

The legend of the origin of Jagan-Natha is peculiar. A hunter killed Krishna, and his body was left to rot under a tree, but some pious person found the bones and placed them in a box. A devout king named Indra Dyumna was directed by Vishnu to form an image of Jagan-Nath and place the bones of Krishna inside it. Vishwakarma, the architect of gods, undertook to make the image, on condition of being left quite undisturbed till the work was complete. After fifteen days the king was impatienrt and went to Vishwakarma, who was angry, and left of work before he had made either hands or feet, so that the image has only stumps. Indra Dyumna prayed to Brahma, who promised to make the image famous, and he did so by giving to it eyes and a soul, and by acting as high priest at its consecration.

From about 300 AD this part of Orissa was occupied by the King Yavanas and the image of Jagan-Nath appeared at Puri in about 318 AD, and a temple built at the same time to house the image. A king of the succeeding Kesari dynasty built the present temple around the ancient temple in about 500 AD. which received periodical additions through the centuries, and was enlarged to the present by a king (Ganga Raja) in 1200 AD in expiation for the sin of killing a Brahman.

The sacred enclosure of the temple of Jaga-Nath at Puri is 652 feet long by 630 feet broad, with a stone wall 20 feet high surrounding it. It contains more than 100 temples and shrines, dedicated to Krishna, Vishnu, Shiva, the Sun god and other deities. The tower of the main temple rises to a height of 200 feet, and inside stand the sacred image of Jagan-Nath and his brother and sister. A large diamond gleams on the head of Jagan-Nath. Pilgrims offer fabulous gifts to the temple, and even the Sikh ruler Ranjit Singh when dying bequeathed the Kohi-noor diamond to Jagan-Narth temple.

The temple has a retinue. of 6,000 priests, attendants, warders and guides. A total of 20,000 men, women and children are dependent on the temple. The Lion's Gate of the temple a man of the sweeper caste strikes the pilgrims with his broom to purify them of their sins before entering the temple. He also makes them promise never to disclose the secrets of the temple.

It is a great place of pilgrimage, and regarded as being very meritorious to visit the temple. The idea of pilgrimage is to fulfill a vow, or to implore benefits.

Janamashtami or Krishna Janamshtami

The Janamashtami means the birthday of Lord Krishna, the eighth incarnation of Vishnu. It falls on the eighth day of the dark half of the month of Bhadrapada (August-September). This is one of the greatest Hindu fasts and festivals. Temples are decorated and processions are taken out to depict various aspect of Lord Krishna's life. The day preceding Janamashthami is observed as a fast, terminating at midnight, at which time Krishna was born. In Vrindaban, Mathura and other parts of northern India the festival is celebrated with great splendour. Temples are decorated with fruits and flowers. Special fairs are held and most of the people visit temple on that day. People believe that they will have a happy and prosperous life by observing this fast.

The Divine echo told Kans, maternal uncle of Lord Krishna, that his sister Devaki would give birth to a son, who would kill him. An astrologer also told him that the eighth boy born unto her would be that one. He therefore put his sister Devaki and her husband Vasudev into prison. They were closely watched, each child as it was born, being killed by the king. The eighth child was saved by a miracle and became the hero of the Mahabharata. He (Lord Krishna) killed his uncle and helped the Pandavas against Kauravas to win their kingdom. Lord Krishna also freed Kans's parents from prison along with many innocent prisoners. Mathura's rule was restored to Ugaraesen (father of Kans) once again. People welcomed Ugarsen's rule. Lord Krishna was a great liberator of a common man. It is the celebration of Lord Krishna's birth that gives its name to the Janamashtami day from Janam (birth) and ashtami the eighth.

Jitashthami

Jit means to win long life and ashthami the eighth day of a month. The eighth day of the latter half of the month of Ashwin is observed in Bengal as a fast day by women in the hope of ensuring long life for their babies. Once upon a time there was a very nice king who had no children from the chief queen. He performed many animal sacrifices and got many charms for having children but nothing happened. One day the queen dreamt that she should perform Jitashthami fast by planting banyan tree and worship it in the prescribed form in order to be blessed by god and then give birth to a son.

The queen observed fast and performed puja (worship) in the prescribed manner every month on eighth day of the dark half. The second queen ridiculed her superstitious thinking. The result was that the Jitashhthami god cursed her and her young child died. The chief queen gave birth to a son and advised the second queen to observe the fast and worship in the prescribed manner. She did so and got blessed by the god with a son. In the end they all lived very happily.

Kal-ashthami

The eighth day of the second half of the month of Kartik is observed as a fast in Varanasi and the night is spent in prayers. The story is that - once upon a time there arose a dispute among the gods as to who was the chief. Brahma, Vishnu and Shiva – all of them claimed the honour. Brahma claimed he was the only chief and asked every one to bow to him, as he was the creator of everything. He asked Shiva to bow down his head to him. He was angry and he created Kal Bhairav and asked him to chop of one of the five heads of Brahma. It was immediately done. Shiva then asked Kal Bhairav to go and live at Varanasi. Ever since that time Kal Bhairav has been the presiding deity of that sacred city, and the Hindu inhabitants of the city keep up the day in his honour.

Kartik ki Katha (worship of Goddess Pathwari)

It is considered meritorious to have an early morning bath during the month of Kartik (October-November) and worship goddess Pathwari. Many people take a cold bath during the month and worship the goddess to gain happiness and prosperity in life. There are many stories, but only one story is mentioned here regarding the holy bath in the month of Kartik.

Once a village girl took holy bath during the month of Kartik to gain a beautiful husband and after getting a beautiful husband she kept on taking the bath during the month to gain prosperity. She was from a poor family and used to go out to sell curd and milk. During the month of Kartik she wanted to go early for a holy dip in the river and then sell curd and milk. Her mother-in-law agreed after a great difficulty. Every day she would go to the river and have a bath and then make an image of goddess Pathwari for daily worship. As she had nothing to offer the goddess, she poured the curd and milk on the image of goddess. On reaching home, her mother-in-law demanded money, which she had earned by selling the curd and milk. She told her mother-in-law that she was selling it to a shop and she will get paid at the end of the month. Every day after worship she poured the milk and curd on the image of the goddess.

At the end of the month she filled a bag with sand and kept it in a corner of her house. Her mother-in-law noticed the bag and demanded money from her for the sale of curd and milk during the month. The daughter-in-law was not sure from where to bring the money. The mother-in-law opened the sand bag and found gold coins, jewels and other precious stones. She told the whole story to her mother-in-law and realized that it was all due to the blessing of the goddess and holy bath in the month of Kartik.

Kartika Purnima/Tripuri-Purnima, (October-November).

Kartika Purnima is the greatest day in the year for the followers of Lord Shiva, next to Maha Shivratri. The festival is observed in commemoration of Shiva's victory over the three giants. These giants are said to have inhabited three celestial cities made respectively of gold, silver and iron, which were adjacent to each other and were capable of being moved about in company at the will of the giants. These giants were a constant source of trouble to gods and men. Lord Shiva slew the troublesome tripurasura and utterly destroyed their cities. This festival is observed on the full moon of Kartika and the day preceding the full moon is observed by the devout as a strict fast. It is at this festival that many women especially worship the moon, with a view to the obtaining of such blessings as an offspring, long life and prosperity. The Matsya avatar (incarnation) of Vishnu is also supposed to have taken place on Tripuri-Purnima.

Karva Chauth or Karka Chaturthi

One of the most important fasts for married women is Karva Chauth. It falls on the fourth day of the bright half of Kartik (October). It is observed by all married women to ensure the long lives, good health and prosperity of their husbands. Women fast all day long, without taking even water.

It is customary for women to receive a Karva (an earthen pot with a spout) and presents from her parents' family on that day. Extremely good vegetarian food is prepared. Some of the food is put in one Karva, and water in another. In the evening all the fasting women say prayers to Gods for the well being of their husband and family. When the moon appears, the women say prayers and offer the food and water. After worshipping Goddess Gauri (Parvati) and the moon they eat and drink. This is a very hard fast to observe as it starts before sunrise and ends when they have seen the moon. Many women take water, juice, tea or coffee during the day if they are feeling sick etc. Usually the mother-in-law of a newly wed gets sargi (food) to be eaten before sunrise on the day of the fast. The food they take in the morning is thirst quenching and keeps the body liquids in proper shape.

Just before the moonrise the women dress up with all the signs of married women (bindi etc.) and offer Puja to Goddess Gauri (Parvati) for the well being and prosperity of their husband. Various stories are connected with the fast, but the moral of all the stories is that a wife should do anything to get her husband back or to restore his health and happiness.

In one of the stories, a young girl called Virvati kept the fast and by mistake broke it before seeing the moon. As soon as she started eating her food, the news came that her husband had died. Virvati's mother knew that the mysterious death of her son-in-law was due to her daughter's mistake. She told her that you will meet seven women on way to your father-in-law's house and only the seventh women will bless you. The seventh woman blessed a long life for her husband. On reaching her father-in-law's house she found her husband alive. She made a genuine mistake and therefore she was pardoned by the almighty. After this she observed the fast regularly and made sure to see the moon before breaking the fast.

At the end of the story, a lady standing next to the newly wed exchanges her Karva with her. Then each woman who is fasting and worshipping exchanges her Karva with the lady next to her, seven times saying: 'Take Suhagan (married woman) my Karva', which is slightly raised in her two hands, together with Thaali (plate) on top of it. The other woman says: 'give Suhagan (married woman) your Karva to me'. Then something is left for charity. After finishing the worship, the bride or woman touches the feet of their elders for their blessings.

Khas (Ghas) Shashth Vrat

Khas or Kush/Khus is a grass known also as Bena in Bengal and Shashthi means the sixth day of the bright half of Paush (December-January). It is a fast followed by worship of the goddess presiding over the day and also named Shashthi. In Bengal it is believed that fast and worship on this day brings happiness and prosperity. The story told on this day is that a Brahman daughter-in-law did not work and kept fast on this day, and stealthily ate the food prepared for family gods on this fast day. Unfortunately her child died young and her mother-in-law told her the benefits of the fast, and also about the wish fulfilling goddess. She made her to keep the fast and also to take interest in household work. One day the daughter-in-law was sent out to do household chores, and in her absence her mother-in-law prepared nice food and made preparation for the worship of the goddess as symbolized by the Patai or Bena plant. The daughter-in-law came home she realized her mistake, and joined in the worship ceremony. After that she participated in household work, kept the fast regularly and devotedly worshipped the goddess. The result was that she gave birth to a healthy son and her sin was expiated. Everyone in her neighborhood adopted the worship and fast.

Krishna Janamashthami *see* Janamashthami

Kshetra Vrat (fast)

Kshetra means a field; Kshetra Devi is the fairy of the field. She is worshipped in Bengal on Saturday in the month of October. The story runs that a boy called Bishu lost his father at the age of five. He and his mother lived with his maternal uncle, as they had no one to support them. But the wife of his uncle was a cruel one. She made Bishu as a shepherd and his mother as a menial worker. They always worked hard, but still not allowed to eat one meal a day. They started begging and always worshipped Kshetra Devi. Whenever they ate some food they first offered food to the idol of Kshetera Devi. Inspite of all the hard work, uncle's wife turned Bishu and his mother out of the house. They started living in the open fields without food. One day the goddess of the fields came and gave them some food to eat and some seeds to sow in the fields. After some time they were surprised to see the field full of fine crop quite ready to harvest. The owner of the field was surprised to see his fields and offered his daughter in marriage to Bishu. Bishu and his mother became rich and built a very nice house there.

In the meantime Bishu's uncle and his wife were cursed by the god and became poor. They came to work as labourers in the fields of Bishu and were recognized by him. Bishu told them the secret of his success and told them to worship Kshetra Devi. They repented, and began worshipping Kshetra Devi and became rich and lived happily after that.

Kumbh Mela (pot fete)

Kumbh (pitcher) fair is the largest religious gathering fair in India. Originally it seems to have been a fertility festival in northern India, celebrated on riverbanks. During some astrological combinations, pots (Kumbha) of grain were brought to these centres and dipped into the river, and then sown along with other seeds to ensure a good harvest.

According to a story in the Vishnu Puranas when the gods and demons churned the ocean, a vessel full of Amrita (nectar) of immortality came out of the ocean. The demons stole the pot and ran off with it and rested or spilled nectar at four places (Allahabad, Haridwar, Ujjain and Nasik)

The four cities are sanctified to have Kumbha Mela every three years. The biggest such Mela falls every twelve years when the sun enters Aries and Jupiter is simultaneously in Aquarius, and the most auspicious place for this fair is Allahabad at the confluence of the Ganges and Jamuna. It is known that Emperor Harsha invited Chinese traveller Hiuen Tsang to a Kumbh Mela at Allahabad where he distributed alms to the poor and ascetics of all faiths.

A pilgrimage to the Kumba Mela is regarded very auspicious, and millions of Hindus and ascetics go to the fair to bathe in the holy waters and offer prayers to the gods. Many people go their to bathe and distribute alms to holy men and needy. People believe that a dip in the holy river at that time will wash away all their and their ancestor's sins back to eighty-eight generations.

Ascetics, holy men of all sects visit the Mela, and a conference of Hinduism is held, where learned metaphysical discussions take place. Naked Sadhus go in a big procession, and it is believed that the mere sight of them cleanse one of all sins. Some barren women take the opportunity of rendering osculatory homage to their ash-besmeared organs in the hope of bearing children.

The occasion of the Mela is regarded very auspicious for initiation into various cults of Sadhus/holy men.

Lohri

Lohari, like Basant and Baisakhi, is a seasonal festival chiefly in the Panjab. It falls in mid-January, when the sun touches the southern most point on the ecliptic and the duration of the night is the longest. The word Lohri seems to have originated from the word Loh and Ari, literally meaning iron foe or black foe, suggestive of the long and dreadful cold nights.

A week or so before the Lohri night, young boys and girls go from house to house singing doggerels, and asking for money, sweets and firewood. On the Lohri night bonfires are lit in households and in public streets. While the Lohri fire burns, the superstitious close their eyes and wish for their heart's desire. Small quantities of peanuts, popcorns, parched rice, sesame seeds, gur (raw sugar) and sweets are thrown into the fire as offerings, and also eaten by the people, who sit, sing and gossip around the fire.

The Lohri fire is symbolic of the homage to the sun. It was believed that the flames of the fire at Lohri took their message to the sun for bringing warmth and taking away the cold weather. There is also another version of Lohri that in the olden times human beings lit fires to keep away flesh eating animals and to protect their habitations. The whole village or locality contributed to this communal fire. The Lohri bonfire is symbolic of our old method of protecting ourselves from cold, as well as a form of fire worship. It is at Lohri that couples pray for children, and also in the home where there is a newborn son, or a newly married person the Lohri is celebrated with even more enthusiasm, and sweets made of molasses, sugar and sesame seeds are sent to relatives and friends.

For peasants the Lohri marks the beginning of the new financial year, because on this day they settle the division of the produce of land between themselves and tillers. Lohri is also associated with weddings, and many wedding sings are based on Dulla of Bhatti village a Muslim, who rescued a Hindu girl from her cruel abductors, and adopted the girl and arranged her marriage as though she were his own daughter. From Lohri bonfire in a village, people collect the ashes before sunrise and take it to their homes as a gift from gods.

Lotan Shasthi

Lotan Shasthi falls on the sixth day of the bright half of Shravan (July-August). Here is a story of a Brahman in Bengal who had a son and daughter-in-law and their seven sons. He had a daughter who had three sons. The Brahmans wife always worshipped the goddess and offered her six balls of lotans on the fast day. On one of the fast days she noticed that three balls of lotan were missing. Her daughter-in-law and daughter denied stealing them. The old woman kept quiet and prepared six cream lotans and offered them to the goddess. At the same time seven sons of the daughter-in-law disappeared from the house. She started crying and every one thought that she must have stolen the lotans.

In the meantime goddess appeared and told her never to lie on the fast day and also that it was a serious sin to swear by placing one's hand on one's son and lie. She apologized for her mistake and the goddess pardoned her. She sprinkled water on the daughter-in-law and her sons came back to life. It is believed that those who perform this worship their children have long and prosperous life.

Maha Shiva Ratri *see* **Shivratri**

Mahalya Amavasya

The new moon of the great destruction, is observed as a day for making offerings to the manes of the dead, who, through dying other than a natural death, may not have received the usual death rites. It occurs on the new moon of the month Bhadrapada (September-October) and is observed by all the Hindus. The ceremonies are very similar to the usual annual ceremonies for the dead. Charity in the form of food is very important during this observance. Therefore one should give plenty of food to the needy during the Mahalaya fortnight and all through the year.

Makar Sankrant

This is the day of the transit of the sun at the tropic of Capricorn – which falls on the 12th or 13th of January every year. On that day the sun is said to begin its journey northwards. To the early Aryans living in a cold region, the approach of spring was an occasion of greatest joy, and the commencement of the sun's northward progress could not pass unmarked. On this day, Hindus apply to their bodies gingerly seed pounded on the curry stone and bathe. They offer the seed mixed with sugar to fire, to the manes of their ancestors, to Brahmans, to their family members, friends, relations and acquaintances. It is believed that this six-fold use of seed destroys all sins. This day is said to be the beginning of the day of the gods, and that of the night of the demons. The gifts usually given to the needy, poor and Brahmans are new pots, food for cows, food for priests, raw sugar, sesamum seeds, wool, ghee (butter), cows, clothes etc. In practice people worship the sun and exchange gifts on this day. The sun is one of the three chief deities in the Vedas, as the great source of light and warmth. The message of the sun is the message of light, unity, impartiality, and selflessness. Without the sun life will perish.

In South India sweet pudding and other sweet meats are prepared in every home during Makar Sankrant. Family members get together and brothers renew contacts by giving presents to their married or unmarried sisters. Young girls prepare and offer food to animals and birds. Cows are also worshipped and fed. The festival represents the beginning of the month, and in South India it is called the Pongal. On this day Tamilians cook the newly harvested corn for the first time. People celebrate the day by giving gifts to relations, servants and the poor. Hindus offer oblations to departed ancestors. The festival in South India is connected with agriculture. The first harvest is offered to the god (Pongal), and then the food and clothes are given to the labourers who work for the landlord.

Among Sikhs the festivals is observed by a great fair at Muktsar (Ferozpur), which lasts three days. The worshippers bath in the holy tank called pool of salvation. They listen to the Guru Granth Sahib and the heroic stories of Guru Gobind Singh.

Mangalvaar (Tuesday) ki Katha – I

Tuesday is also devoted to Lord Hanuman. The devotees listen to the following story before breaking their fast in the afternoon. The fast is observed for gaining royal patronage, happiness, and prosperity or for getting a son. People listen to the story before breaking the fast. People usually wear red clothes at worship and offer red flowers to the deity. Lord Hanuman is also worshipped on this day. Once an old lady worshipped Mangal deity or Mars. She kept fast on Tuesday to propitiate the deity. The lady had a son called Mangal as he was born on Tuesday. The deity tested the old lady and realized that she had unquestioned faith in the deity and promised to her that she will never face any difficulty in life.

Some wrestlers observe Tuesday as a rest day. Once there was an old lady who used to keep Tuesday in honor of Lord Hanuman. She used to get four loaves from her daughter-in-law every day to eat. On Tuesday she would give two loaves to the Hanuman temple. Her daughter-in-law stopped giving her loaves, but Lord Hanuman disguised as a child gave her house and all the necessities she required to live. In the meantime her son, his wife and children became ill and very poor, as they did not believe in Lord Hanuman.

They realized their mistake and begged the old lady to come back home. As soon as the old lady came back to her family house every one became healthy and prosperous. They all became prosperous and started keeping Tuesday fast in honor of Lord Hanuman.

Mangalvaar (Tuesday) ki Katha – II

Once there was a couple that had no children. The husband went away to earn some money and the wife kept Tuesday fast to appease Lord Hanuman. Thee Lord was very pleased with her devotion and he blessed her with a beautiful son. After some time the husband returned home and saw a beautiful boy who called him Daddy. He became suspicious and thought that his wife had obtained son from some one else. She told her husband that she kept Tuesday fast and Lord Hanumans had blessed her with a son. Lord Hanuman appeared in his dream and told him that he had blessed his wife with a son. He realized his mistake kept Tuesday fast regularly with his wife and they became very happy and prosperous.

Naag Panchami ki Katha

Naag-Panchami (meaning snake-fifth). Naag – a snake, especially cobra-capella. A mythical semi-divine being, having a human face with a tail of a serpent. Special worship is offered to snakes on Naag Panchamui, The festival is observed on the fifth day of the light half of Shriven (July-August), commemorating the victorious return of Krishna from the Yamuna after he overcame the serpent Kaliya. People keeps fast on that day and bathing fairs are held on the banks of holy rivers. Pictures of Seshnaagh (mythological naagas) are worshipped. The real object may be for the masses are to be preserved from being bitten by snakes; but there is also some idea that the poison of snakes is able to cure certain diseases. The Nag is considered demi-god and is supposed to be malevolent and, therefore, much of the worship is for the purpose of deprecating their wrath.

One of the stories regarding the fast says that a Brahman had seven daughter-in-laws. All of them used to visit their parents except the youngest, which had lost them. She used to say that Naag king (Sheshnaag) the thousand-hooded snake on whose coil sleeps Lord Vishnu, was her relation and protector. The Naag king was moved to pity by her statement. He assumed the shape of an old Brahman and went to claim the girl as her niece. He took her to his kingdom where she had nice holidays. On the fifth day of the month of Shravan (July-August) she worshipped snakes for the welfare of those cobras that got deformed by her mistakes during her holidays with Shesh Naag Due to her prayers the deformed cobras got restored to normal life. They offered her jeweled necklace and she became very prosperous. Every one listen to the story before breaking the fast. People offer milk to the snakes and some also visit snake holes to offer them milk. Snake charmers collect money to feed the snakes.

Another story says that a farmer while ploughing his field crushed to death some young cobras. The mother of the cobras went to avenge the daughter of the farmer who has killed young cobras. At that time the daughter was worshipping the Shesh Naag and praying for the welfare of the young cobras. The mother went back to her hole and found all the young cobras got restored to normal life by the prayers of that farmer's daughter. Since then it has been ruled that on the fifth day of the Shravan there shall be no ploughing operation and Shesh Naag and other snakes should be fed with milk.

Navaratra

The great Navaratra ceremony begins on the first day of Ashwin (September-October). Nav means nine and ratra means night. It lasts for nine days in honour of nine manifestations of goddess (Devi). In Bengal the clay image of Devi (Durga) is worshipped for nine days and on the tenth day the image is immersed in a nearby river. The nine nights are sacred to Devi (goddess), whose ten manifestations and several exploits are mentioned in the Devi Mahatmaya of the Markandeya Purana.

In her milder form she is Uma (light and a type of beauty), Gauri (yellow or brilliant), Parvati (mountaineer and Himavati from her parentage), Jagat-mata (mother of the world) and Bhavani.

In her terrible form she is Durga (the inaccessible), Kali (the black), Chandi (the fierce), and Bhairvi (the terrible). It is in this character the bloody sacrifices are offered to her during Durga Puja. She has ten arms and in most of her hands she has weapons. As Kali or Kalika (black), she is represented with a black skin, face dripping with blood, encircled with snakes, hung round with skull and heads of demons. As Vindhya-vasini (dweller in Vindhyas), she is worshipped at Mirzapur where Vindhyas approach the Ganges. As a Durga she rides on a tiger in a fierce and menacing attitude. She is renowned slayer of demons, and is actually supposed to be goddess Kali. She killed Mahisha (buffalo demon), demons Sumbha and Nisumbha. She also killed demon Raktavija (blood sprinkling demon – as each drop of his blood had the power to become a demon), and Tripurasura.

In the Chandi–mahatmya, which celebrate the victories of this goddess (Devi) over the Asuras (demons), speaks of her under the following names: (1) Durga, when she received the messengers of the Asuras. (2) Dasa-bhuja (ten armed), when she destroyed part of their army. (3) Sinha-vahini (riding on a lion), when she fought with demon's general Rakata-vija. (4) Mahisha-mardini (destroyer of Mahish (demon) in the form of a buffalo. (5) Jagad-dhatri (foster of the world), when she defeated again the demon army. (6) Kali (the black) She killed Rakta-Vijay, (blood sprinkling demon – as each drop of his blood had the power to become a demon). (7). Mukta-kesi (disheveled hair) – again defeat the demons. (8) Tara (star), she killed Sumbha demon. (9) Chhinna-mastaka. Decapitated, the headless form in which she killed Nisumbha demon. (10) Jagad-gauri (world's fair one), as lauded by gods for her triumphs.

On the first day of the month of Ashwin (September-October), a water pot is placed on an alter. The eighth day is observed as a feast, and on the ninth, the sacred fire is kindled. Animal sacrifices are offered to her. An unmarried girl is worshipped. When the moon arrives at the constellation called Mula, she is invited to come, and when at the constellation Shravan (July-August) she is allowed to return to her heavenly abode. On the Vijay Dashmi day, she is worshipped again before finally bidding her good bye. During the nine days of Navratra, her devotees either fast or take only one meal. If they are unable to do so, they observe the fast for seven, five or three days, at least. Brahmans and poor people are fed and given cash and clothes. The unmarried girls selected to, represent the goddess, should be healthy, beautiful, and free from eruptions. It is advisable to worship nine girls simultaneously on the fifth day of the month, when the goddess Lalita is especially worshipped.

The origin of the Navaratra is thus given. When Rama found that as soon as he cut off any heads of Ravan, they came to life again. Ravana had ten heads representing: passion, pride, anger, greed, infatuation, lust hatred, jealousy, selfishness and crookedness of the demon ego, and thus justly celebrating Dussehra. In northern and western India Navaratra also forms a part of Dussehra.

All the gods became alarmed at this phenomenon and prayed to goddess Devi. She awoke at midnight of the first day of Ashwin (September-October) and blessed Rama – that he would be able to kill Ravana. The gods were grateful and decided to fast and worship the goddess. They performed Puja (worship) in the best possible way, and Rama killed Ravana on the eighth day. The goddess appeared before the gods and they ignited the sacred fire on the ninth day and offered sacrifices. On the tenth day Rama started back triumphantly for his capital and therefore this day is called Vijay Dashami or Dussehra (Vijay means success and

Dashami means the tenth day). Before taking his seat in the heavenly vehicle, Rama worshipped the Shami tree (Prosopis spicigera), and then went to heaven.

Lord Shiva permitted his wife Parvati, daughter of Himavant (Himalayas) to go and see her mother only during these nine days (Navaratra) once a year, after which her mother had to send her back. The women make images to which they attach themselves like a mother to her daughter, whom she has to let go to her husband.

Navaratre *see* **Durga Puja and Dussehra**

Parshuram Jayanti

He was the first Ram and the sixth incarnation of Vishnu. He was known as the Ram with the axe. He was a Brahman, the fifth son of sage Jamadagani and Renuka (Kashatriya princess). His mother Renuka, went to her sister's house, which was the queen of king Sahasarjun. She was not respected there. Jamadagani got annoyed with her and ordered Parshuram to cut off the head of his mother. He did that, and the father was pleased and told him to ask a boon. He begged his father to restore his mother to life, and for himself that might be invincible in single combat and enjoy a long life. It was done and she became alive.. It is said that Kashatriyas killed Jamadagani, and in retaliation Parshuram carried on twenty-one expeditions against the Kashatriyas. In the end he got defeated by Lord Ram. His birthday is observed, as a fast day, on the second moon of Vaisakh (April-May), especially by Brahmans whom he helped, when there was a great rivalry between the ruling class and the priestly class.

Pole Ceremonies

A number of Hindu festivals were associated with the erection of poles, which were ceremonially set up and often worshipped. The Dhvaja aropana (pole planting) a rite of great antiquity is the reminiscent of the erection of the Maypole in Europe. It was usually celebrated on the first day of the light half of Chaitra (March-April). A tall slender tree was felled, its trunk smoothed and the pole set up in the middle of the village. It was decorated with a garland of leaves and flowers and surmounted by a flag. The pole was worshipped with offerings and dances to keep away the evil spirits, and after four days it was pulled down and thrown into a river.

Other popular festivals, such as Holi, included pole erecting, but the most important of these was the Indra-dhvaja-puja (Indra's banner worship). It is said that when the first drama, depicting the churning of the ocean, was enacted by the gods and nymphs in honour of Indra, the demons tried to disrupt the festivities, but Indra taking the staff of his banner beat them and drove them away. In commemoration of that event the sage Bharata prescribed the decoration and worship of Indra's flagstaff as a preliminary to the performance of any play, and the dhvaj (flag) was displayed as an emblem of good luck at all theatrical performances.

Pradosha Vrata (fast)

The Pradosha worship is to be performed in the evening twilight on the thirteenth day of each lunar fortnight. . It is the worship of Lord Shiva and Parvati for victory and success in all undertakings and desires. The Skanda Puran relates how Sandila Muni (sage) prescribed the Vrat to a Brahman lady with two princes (Suchivrata and Dharmagupta). Their father was slain and kingdom taken by the enemies. The woman and the boys performed the fast with great devotion. After four months Lord Shiva was pleased with their devotion and one prince (Suchitra) got a pot of nectar and drank the divine ambrosia. At the same time Dharmagupta got married to celestial princess as recommended by Lord Shiva. Due to Pradosha Vrat Lord Shiva was pleased and the help of the Lord restored the kingdom to them.

On the fast day devotees should worship Lord Shiva, Parvati, Ganesh Skanda and Nandi. After the worship, Pradosh story is read and heard by the devotees. Some gifts of food and clothes are given to poor Brahman and needy people. This fast is highly recommended by the scriptures and is of great importance to the devotees of Lord Shiva. The Vrat destroy all sins and Lord showers his blessings to the devotees. In some temples and Ashrams in India, a special Havan and an elaborate worship are conducted for the long life, health, success and prosperity of every one in this world.

Rakhi or Raksha Bandhan

Rakhi falls in July-August and is observed on the full moon day of the month of Srawan (July-August). Hindus and Sikhs observe the festival all over the world. Rakhi is also known by some other names for example, Rakhari and Solono, The word Solono is a corruption of the Persian word Sal-I-Nai (new near), and it is a name given to the full moon of Srawan/Sawan, because it marks the point of transition between the old and the new agriculture year.

Rakhi means tying an ornamental cord round the wrist of brother or other male relative. The silk or cotton cord is called Raksha because it is intended to serve as an amulet guarding the wearer from all kinds of evils. These are usually died in yellow or red; but very often they are blazoned with variety of gaudy colours and ornamented with tassels, to suit individual tastes. After the ceremony a tilak is applied on the forehead of brother and a piece of sweetmeat in his mouth. In return the brother gives her some gift.

In olden days Raksha Bandhan/Rakhi was a Brahman festival. This is based on an ancient saying which enumerates four chief denominational festivals, corresponding to the four chief divisions of the Hindus. The Raksha is the festival for Brahmans, Dussehra for Kshatriyas, Diwali for Vaishyas and Holi for Shudras.

In some towns, in ancient times, Brahmans of the priestly order wander about the town all day, carrying a bundles of

Raksha Bandhan threads and visiting rich people's houses, tying a Raksha thread on their wrists and receiving cash payment in return.

The legend connected with the origin of the festival is as follows:

Once Yudhishtra inquired from Krishna as to how impending evils could be warded off throughout the year. Krishna advised him to observe Raksha Bandhan in consonance with the scriptures. He also narrated to him a story of a long-drawn series of battles between Indra and demon king. Indra was defeated and driven away from his kingdom. God Brihaspati advised Indra to wait for the most opportune time of the full moon day of Srawan to attack the demon king. Indrani and Brihaspati tied a Rakhi each around the right hand wrist of Indra. After the ceremony Indra attacked the demon king, defeated him, and re-established his superiority over Trilok (all the three worlds) – heaven, earth and hell.

At the time of tying a Rakhi thread, the following couplet is uttered. Thus I tie the thread around your wrist – the same that was twined round the arms of the mighty Bali (king of Danavas). May the protection afforded by it be eternal.

At present, instead of a Brahman, a sister or sisters tie Rakhi on the right wrist of their brothers, applies a tilak on forehead, and put some piece of sweetmeat in his mouth. In return the brother gives her some money or gift. This is symbolic of sister asking for brother's protection and the latter promising it. Where sisters cannot go and tie Rakhi personally, they send it by post. Sometimes Brahmans also visit their patrons and present Rakhi in return for cash payment. Rakhi is also celebrated by a large majority of Sikhs.

In South India – Raksha Bandhan is called Avani Avittam. Hindus wear a new holy thread and offer libations of water to their ancestors and ancient Rishis on this day. Recitations of Vedas on this day are highly beneficial to everyone.

Ramnaumi or Sri Ramanaumi

On the first of Chaitra (March-April) begins the celebration of the birth of Lord Ram (seventh incarnation of Vishnu). Stories from Ramayana are narrated and Rama is worshipped. Large quantities of food are distributed to the poor people. Every evening sermons are delivered by professional priests in all temples dedicated to Ram until the ninth day, when as soon as the sun reaches the meridian, the birth is celebrated with great éclat. In many temples Ramnaumi is celebrated for nine days and devotees reads Ramayana during these nine days.

Ramayana is the oldest of the Sanskrit epic poems, written by Valmiki. Ramayana celebrates the life and exploits of Rama, the loves of Rama and his wife Sita, the abduction of Sita by Ravana (demon king of Ceylon), the war carried on by Rama and his devotee Hanuman and his army against Ravana, ending in the destruction the demon king and the rescue of Sita, the restoration of Rama to the throne of Ayodhya, his jealousy and banishment of Sita, her residence at the hermitage of Valmiki, the birth of her twin sons (Kusa and Lava), the father's discovery and recognition of his children, the recall of Sita, the attestation of her innocence, her death, Rama's resolution to follow her, and his translation to heaven.

The origin of the Navaratri is thus given. When Rama found that as soon as he cut off any heads of Ravan, they came to life again. All the gods became alarmed at this phenomenon and prayed to goddess Devi. She awoke at midnight of the first day of Ashwin (September-October) and blessed Rama – that he would be able to kill Ravana. The gods were grateful and decided to fast and worship the goddess. They performed Puja (worship) in the best possible way, and Rama killed Ravana on the eighth day. The goddess appeared before the gods and they ignited the sacred fire on the ninth day and offered sacrifices. On the tenth day Rama started back triumphantly for his capital and therefore this day is called Vijay Dashami or Dussehra (Vijay means success and Dashami means the tenth day).

Ratha Saptami

Ratha Saptami falls on the 7th day of the bright fortnight of the month of Margaseersha (December-January). People worship the sun the morning and recite the Surya Sahasarnam. The Sun god is one of the three chief deities mentioned in the Vedas, as the great source of light and warmth. In Atharva Veda Surya (Sun God) has cosmogonic significance; he surveys the whole world, sees beyond the sky, the earth and the primordial waters, from him may derives his visionary facilities. He possesses curative powers and thus is the preserver of life.

Virtuous actions done on this day give manifold beneficial results. All those who worship the Sun god on this day, observe a vow of silence are sure to attain salvation.

Ravivaar (Sunday) = Surya Naraayan (Sun God) fast ki Katha) I.

People keep fast on Sunday in the name of the Sun God. Food is taken only once a day, generally fruit before sunset. Many people do not take saltish and fried food. It is believed that fast on Sunday saves one from skin diseases, ringworm and eye sores. The story is described as follows:

Once the Sun God ruled the world. He fed half a spoon of food to every one on earth and the other half of spoon to his family. The Sun God's wife was not happy with half a spoon of food. She wanted more food for herself and her family. The God did not want to give more food unless they work for it. The wife of God went to a neighbor's house to pass time, but the lady said that she had no time to sit with her as she was fasting on Sunday, and busy cleaning the house and preparing food for worship. The lady said that she always wake up early, work hard, clean the house and pray to the Sun God for our welfare and health. She advised the Sun God's wife to fast on Sunday, work hard, clean your house and eat fruit or rice before sun-set and avoid salty and fried food. The wife of God took advice and kept fast on all Sundays and then she became happy and prosperous in a very short time. After that the Sun God and his family led a happy and prosperous life.

Ravivaar (Sunday) Sun and the Divine Cow ki Katha - II.

This story of the Sun God is also told on Sunday fast. It depicts the importance of cow and cow dung and suggests the victory of innocence over jealousy.

Once an old lady lived a happy life. She would get up early in the morning and took her bath and kept her house clean by plastering with cow dung from her neighbor. She took her food only after offering food to the Sun God. The neighbor refused to give her cow dung. The Sun God was pleased with her Sunday fast and gave her a beautiful cow that gave gold dung. As the news spread the king ordered his army to bring the cow to him. The king had a bad dream of his mistake and returned the divine cow to the old lady. The king proclaimed that all his subjects should observe fast on Sundays in honor of the Sun God if they wanted their desire to be fulfilled. After that all his people became healthy and prosperous by observing Sunday fast.

Sakranti

Sakranti, or the commencement of the sun's northern course in the heavens, occurs in the month of Pushya (December-January). This feast is called Pongal in the south, and is the commencement of the Tamil year. It is a harvest festival last for three days. On the first day houses are cleaned, oil is rubbed on the body and a bath is taken. On the second and third day gods are worshipped and carried in procession.

Samvatsaradi

Samvatsaradi is the festival of the New Year. The Telugu New Year's day is the first day of the month Chaitra (March-April) and is observed by all the Hindus. This is not a religious festival; this seems to be analogous to the English idea that it is necessary to eat good food on the day.

Sankat Chauth Vrat (fast)

Sankat Chauth falls in the month of Magh (January-February). It is believed that the position between the sun and moon is such that it disturbs balanced thinking. A fast on this day keep the mind in balance. Once there was a pious lady who used to keep the fast for the welfare of her very hard working son. Some people in the village were jealous of her good living due to the fast. Some villagers misguided her son about her intentions towards him. The son came back after working in the fields and told her mother that he was going to the city for a better life. His mother was not happy about her son's decision, but assured him that she will keep on observing the fast for his welfare, but in case of any difficulty in his journey, she gave him some barley and sesame seeds. She told her son that in difficult times he should scatter them in front of him to save him from bad happenings. He was passing through the jungle when a hungry lion came roaring towards him. He immediately remembered the advice of his mother and scattered barley in front of him. The lion looked at him and ran away. After a little while he has to cross a flooded river. He scattered some barley in front of him and jumped into the river and crossed it safely. At nighttime he saw a hut where an old lady was crying and cooking food for his son. He asked her for shelter and enquired why she was crying. The lady said that tomorrow morning is her son's turn to give sacrifice to our king for the prosperity of his kingdom. . The boy told the lady to give him food to eat and he will offer himself to the king for sacrifice in place of her son.

The lady agreed reluctantly and the boy enjoyed the food and had a sound sleep. Next morning the boy went to the king's palace where he was asked to lie down on a sacrificial platform. The boy remembered his mother's advice and spread barley and sesame around him to save his life. Due to some miracle the king could only see Lord Krishna lying there instead of the sacrificial boy. The king realized that he was misguided about the sacrifice and offered apologies to the boy.

The boy told the whole story to the king about his mother's pious devotion towards the fast, and advised the king to offer only bloodless offering of food to gods, such as butter, fruit, grains along with prayers to remove obstacles and for the welfare and prosperity of his kingdom. He also told the king that Mandala Upanishad declares that human sacrifices are sinful and evil, and the fools who cling to them go to hell. No one can obtain religious, moral or worldly happiness by human sacrifice.

The king immediately stopped the human sacrifice and ordered his subject to keep fast on all four days of Sankat Chauth, and offer only bloodless offering of food to gods, such as butter, fruit, grains along with prayers to remove obstacles and for welfare and prosperity.

He thanked the boy for his advise and happily married one of his daughter's to him. The king gave him a lot of money and sent him back to his mother. The boy brought his wife to his mother and begged her blessing for the happiness and prosperity of all of them.

Satya Narayan Vrat (fast)

Once Divine sage Narad, son of Brahma, came to earth from heaven and saw people very miserable and suffering in according to their Karma (actions). He was unable to help in relieving them from their sufferings. He went back to heaven and requested Lord Narayan (Satya Narayan) to tell him the easiest way to relieve earthly people from their sufferings and from this cycle of birth and death. Lord Narayan told Narad that people should observe the Satya Narayan fast on the full moon day, in the months of kartik, Vaisakh, Sravan and Chaitra Purnima and Shankranti day. It can also be done on new moon days. The fast (Vrat) gives relief from pain and distress and grants a copious supply of food and wealth. It also bestows long life to the husbands of married women, gives them children, and grants success in every undertaking. It should be performed in company with relations, friends and Brahmans in the afternoon. God Narayan should be worshipped and to him should be offered a pie made from one and a quarter seers of flour or one and a quarter of any measure, mixed with sliced plantations, ghi, milk and sugar. . But every one of these ingredients should be "one and a quarter" in measure or weight. This katha (story) should then be read aloud, and all the Brahmans, relations and guests should be fed. During this Kali Yuga (Iron Age), this is the easiest way of attaining success in everything.

Five stories are connected with this fast. They speak the glory of Satya Narayan, His Grace and His prasad (sacred food) and devotees derive tremendous benefits by observing the fast. He who hears the stories of the Vrat with faith, devotion and love, derives many benefits. The following stories connected with this fast and the first one is the story of Narad, already stated above. The other four stories have great moral lessons in them concerning truthfulness, fulfillment of promises etc.

The story of a poor Brahman. There was a poor Brahman from Varanasi who lived on alms. Seeing his poor state the Lord appeared in the form of a Brahman and asked why he beg and wander in such a painful state. The poor man explained his poor state and prayed that he be shown the way to get out of the clutches of poverty. He suggested to him to observe the Satya Narayan Vrat to be free from poverty. He then explained the process and disappeared. On that he got a lot of money from begging and kept the fast,

Narayan Vrat. He instructed him to keep the fast to get rid of all the worries from their lives. The ascetic revealed his true identity and blessed the merchant and disappeared. He came back to his boat and found all the jewels and diamonds safe in bags.

After a few days the merchant and his son-in-law reached on the bank of a river near his town and sent a message to his wife and daughter of their arrival. At that time they were hearing Satya Narayan Katha. Immediately after finishing worship they forgot to take prasad (sacred food) and went to receive them. Lord Satya Narayan was annoyed that they did not take prasad. So the boat became invisible with diamonds and the son-in-law. The merchant heard a divine echo that your wife has not taken the sacred food before leaving the place of worship, and therefore the boat has become invisible. He told his wife and daughter to go back, and take prasadam (sacred food) and then return to receive us. After taking prasadam, mother and daughter returned and they found the boat, son-in-law and jewels etc safe. The merchant narrated the whole story of their travels and misfortunes and how the Lord saved them. After that all the family members observed the Satya Narayan vrat regularly during Purnima and Sankrant and lived happily. After death they all went to heaven.

The story of King Tungadhwaja. There was once a king named Tungadhwaja – very kind, generous and always ready to protect his subject. He was also made to suffer for not accepting prasadam (sacred food) of Satya Narayan vrat. One day he had gone to the forest on a shooting excursion. Due to heat he sat under a banyan tree. Some cowherds were engaged in Satya Narayan puja. The king saw them but did not go to take part in the worship. The cowherd after puja took some prasadam (sacred food) to him. He cast a look of contempt at the offering and returned to his capital. The result was that for this gross insult to the sacred food the king was made to see his hundred sons disappear at once. He lost his wealth and realized his mistake. He therefore went to cowherds, and in their company worshipped Satya Narayan, partook of sacred food with them. The Lord was pleased and the king regained his lost sons, and his lost wealth. He enjoyed happy life and in the end he went to heaven.

He who performs this vrat with real devotion, he who hears this wish-fulfilling story, gets by the grace of god Satya Narayan, wealth, health and happiness. Worshippers of this god get whatever they wish and there is no doubt that they reach heaven after death.

Shanivaar = Saturday (Saturn) fast ki Katha – I

Once upon a time a Brahman used to help the king against evil spirits. One day he heard a strange voice saying that it wants to harm the king. He told the voice to harm him rather than the king, as he is responsible for the whole kingdom. The voice or the spirit was pleased with the Brahman's offer. In the meantime two princes went hunting and got lost. The king blamed the Brahman for the loss of his sons. Fortunately the Brahman brought them back to the palace safely. The strange voice told the king not to harm the Brahman and if you wish to be saved from the Saturn (Shanivaar Devta) you must donate a lot of money to charity on Saturday. The strange voice asked the king to announce that the middle-income people should donate black blankets and iron and the poor people should give oil-touched loaf to a black dog on Saturdays. Some people can water a Peepal tree. In general people should see their face in the oil pot and put some money in the pot of the beggar on Saturdays.

Usually the story is related on Saturday fast. Devotees worship Saturn idol made of iron. Black flowers, sesame seeds, horse beans (Urd daal) and black clothes are used for worship. Black article and clothes are also given in donation. Black see same seeds and horse beans (Urd daal) are taken as food on Saturday fast. Wives do not undertake journeys to their paternal homes. The Saturday fast keep away all the hurdles and misfortunes. It is believed that Saturn sits in a mirror chariot, yoked with eight black horses.

Shanivaar = Saturday (Saturn) fast ki Katha – II

During Saturday fast people massage their bodies with mustard oil and give oil in charity to keep off the influence of the Saturn. In the afternoon fasting people eat parched grain after hearing one or the other story.

Another story dealing with the fast is that once the seven deities of the seven days of the week and Rahu and Ketu were sitting together and discussing as to who was the most powerful amongst them. Lord Indra suggested to them to go to the wise king Vikramaditya (ruler of the earth) for the answer. The king did not want to offend any one by telling as to who was the most powerful. Therefore he arranged five beautiful chairs made of gold, silver, bronze, brass, tin, zinc, mica and iron. He asked all the seven to sit on a chair of their choice. The Sun sat on the golden chair and the Saturn sat on the iron chair. The king said that you could decide your own rank according to your chair. The Saturn got annoyed with the king and pointed out that he has ranked him the lowest amongst the deities and cursed him to live poorly the life of a handicapped man. When the king became poor and handicapped person, he started keeping Saturday fast in honor of the Saturn. . The Saturn was pleased with his devotion and respect towards him and soon made him a healthy, wise and powerful king. The king declared in his kingdom that Saturn was equally powerful compared to other deities. He will become prosperous and healthy who so ever will keep fast on Saturday and feed the ants in the morning and evening in honor of Saturn.

Shanivaar = Saturday (Saturn) fast ki Katha – III

This story is about the worship of Peepal tree. There were two sisters called Lakshmi and Daridra. Lakshmi was the goddess of wealth and happiness and Daridra was the goddess of poverty and laziness. Lakshmi was liked by Lord Krishna and got married to him. Daridra was always lazy and could not find a husband. With the help of her sister Lakshmi and Lord Krishna she was married to a Rishi. The Rishi threw her out as she proved to be very lazy, unclean and did not follow the rules of Rishi's hermit. Lakshmi requested Lord Krishna to find a suitable abode for her sister Daridra. He agreed and found a Peepal tree as her abode and told her that it will suit this lonely place to a lazy person like her. On her request Lord Krishna and Lakshmi agreed to visit her on every Saturday at the Peepal tree. Many people water and offer prayers to the tree on Saturday knowing that Lord Krishna and Lakshmi are there on that day.

Shankara Jayanti (788-838)

Shankara's Jayanti (birth) falls on the fifth day of the bright half of Vaisakh (May-June).

He was the founder of the School of Monastic philosophy. His father Nambudri Brahmin was very old when Shankara was born. On his birthday some people fast, many study his works, pray and meditate and get showered with his blessings. He was a great religious reformer and teacher of Vedanta philosophy, was a native of Malabar, born in Kaladi (Travancore), and lived a very erratic life, disputing with heretics and popularizing the Vedanta philosophy by his preaching and writings wherever he went. His travels extended as far as Kashmir and he died at the age of thirty-two. His learning and sanctity were held in such high estimation and reverence, that he was looked upon as an incarnation of Shiva, and was believed to have the power of working miracles. Lord Shiva was the special object of his worship, and he was the founder of the great sect of Smartava Brahmans, who are very numerous and powerful in the south. He established several monasteries for the teachings and preservation of his doctrines. The chief one is at Sringiri, on the edge of the Western Ghauts in the Mysore, and it has the supreme control of Smartava sect. The writings attributed to him are numerous; chief among them are his commentaries on the Sutras or aphorisms of Vyas, a commentary on the Bhagvad Gita, some commentaries on Upanishads, and the Ananda-Lahiri, a hymns in praise of Parvati (wife of Shiva).

Sharad Purnima Vrat

The Vrat (fast) falls on the full moon day of Ashvin (September-October) and devotees who keep the fast prepare kheer (rice and milk pudding) to eat at midnight in the moonlight. It is believed that Lord Krishna used to perform Ras Lila (special dance) with his Gopis on this night.

The story of the fast is that there were two sisters, the elder sister was a pious woman and she always kept Sharad Purnima fast for the welfare of her family. The younger sister kept the fast occasionally half-heartedly. The elder sister lived happily with her children and the younger sister's children kept on dying after birth.

The older sister advised the younger sister to keep the fast with dedication and your next child will survive. She took the advise of her sister and carefully performed the puja on the full moon day of Ashvin and started observing the fast. The result was that all her wishes were fulfilled and became rich. Soon she gave birth to a very healthy child. She told every one that her elder sister was a goddess, and the people of the town started respecting her like a goddess. All her friends also became rich and happy by worshipping and keeping fast on the full moon day of Ashvin.

Sheetala Devi (Goddess of Smallpox) ki Katha

Sheetala Devi is worshipped in March/April on the first Monday after Holi. People eat one-day-old cold food to avoid an attack of smallpox, boils or measles.

There was a wise old lady who always ate cold food and bathed in cold water. People called her Sheetal (cool). She believed that sleeping under the shadow of a Neem or some other tree and eating cold food makes one free from smallpox and many other diseases. Once fire broke out in the village and all the houses caught fire except her house. She told everyone that she always kept fast in honor of the goddess on Sheetal Saptami, and due to her blessing her house did not catch fire. Since then many people of all religions keep fast on Sheetal Saptami day and take cold food to avoid smallpox and other diseases.

Shivratri

Shivratri is a day of fasting in honor of Lord Shiva. It falls on the thirteenth day of each half of the month and is a full day (24 hours) fast. *Maha Shivratri* which falls in the month of Magh (January-February) is considered especially sacred. This day is observed to show mercy and kindness to domestic and wild animals and all other creatures. On Shivratri night the Shiva Ling is worshipped from dusk to dawn by pouring over it milk, curd, honey and rose water, while the Mantra (Om Namah Shivai Namah) is recited. Hymns glorifying Shiva are sung, notably the Shiva Mahima Stotra by Pushpadanta, and the Shiva Tantra Stotra by Ravana. Whoever repeats the name of Shiva during Shivratri with devotion is freed from all sins.

The Linga is the most prominent symbol to represent Lord Shiva. Many ancient cultures (Egyptians and Greeks) worshipped a god with a phallus (Linga). Ancient Egypt had two: Geb and Min (whom the Greeks knew as Priapus). Osiris himself is shown with his phallus erect while he is lying in his coffin. The Lingam is often seen in India in the shape of a pillar with a hemispherical top, standing in a basin or a round tank called yoni.

A brief story about the Shivling is mentioned below. There was a Shivling temple next to a pond in the midst of a forest surrounded by Bilva trees. The Bilva (vilva, bel, Aegle Marmelos) or wood apple has a triple leaf and is sacred to Shiva and a part of Shiva resides in its leaves. It is forbidden to break its branches and it is not to be used for firewood.

Many animals used to come to drink water from the pond next to Shivling. Many hunters used to come to the forest to hunt animals. One day a hunter followed the track of antelopeand hid himself on top of a Bilva tree next to the Shivling pond. Earlier he had heard people chanting Shiva, Shiva, and he also kept on chanting Shiva, Shiva while waiting for some animal. Soon night fell and no animal appeared and during the night on the tree he felt cold and started chanting Shiva, Shiva again while waiting for some animals. Unknowingly he plucked the Bilva tree leaves and threw them on the ground where there was a Shivling. He continued plucking up and throwing the leaves at the Lingam. The result was that one-fourth part of his accumulated sins had disappeared, as the leaves are the most favourite of Lord Shiva.

All of a sudden he saw three antelopes and he caught them. The antelopes said to the hunter not to kill them as they had come in search of food for their young ones. After feeding our young ones we will come back. The hunter took pity on them and let them go away on the condition that they will come back to him. In the meantime Lord Shiva in the form of an ascetic appeared and told the hunter that it is sinful and evil to kill and eat animals, and the fools who do that go to hell. No one can obtain worldly happiness by killing animals and eating them. The hunter felt ashamed and asked for forgiveness. The ascetic blessed him happiness and told him to be merciful to animals. The hunter vowed not to hunt in future and would lead a pious life.

After feeding their young ones all the three antelopes came back to the hunter with their young ones. He collected some grass and gave them to eat and asked them to go back from where they came. Soon after Lord Shiva's messenger arrived and told the hunter that they were deputed to take the hunter's purified soul to Shiva's abode. The antelopes and their families were also taken to heaven.

Lord Shiva told Parvati that you could see in the sky the path (the milky way) by which antelopes went to their

Skanda Sashti falls in November. It is the day on which Lord Subrahmanya defeated the demon Taraksurya. On this day elaborate festivals are held. Devotees worship the lord and prayer meetings are held in many different temples and private residences. Many incurable diseases are cured if one visits Palanni and worship Lord Subrahmanya there. In South India Lord's stories are dramatized on the stage. Devotees also observe weekly and monthly days in His honour. Every Friday, or the Kartigai Nakshatram day every month, or the sixth day of the bright fortnight – all these are sacred days for the devotees. The sixth day of the month of Tulam (October-November) is the most auspicious of them all. This is the Skanda Sashti day.

In many places the festival commences six days prior to the Sashti itself and concludes on the day of the Sashti. During these days, devotees recite various hymns and read stories connected with Lord Subrahmanya, and visit various shrines connected with the Lord. The Lord blesses the devotees with peace, bliss and prosperity.

Somvaar (Lord Shiva – the Deity of Monday) ki Katha – I

Monday fast is kept in honor of Lord Shiva. It has a special significance in the month of Shravan (July-August). Vegetarian food is taken once a day in the afternoon. It is believed that the fast brings prosperity, happiness and learning to the family.

Once a poor Brahman had no money to feed his family. At the request of his wife he started on a long journey to earn some money. In a Jungle he raised a platform around the Peepal tree and meditated there for 12 years. The travellers used to offer him food. Lord Shiva was pleased with his prayers and Monday fasts. The Lord disguised himself as an ascetic with a staff in his hand and blessed the Brahman. The Brahman asked him some financial help. The ascetic gave him a Mantra for his prosperity. The ascetic said that the Mantra is – that Tuesday, Wednesday, Thursday, Friday,

Saturday and Sunday are connected with one or the other deity, and Lord Shiva is the deity of Somvaar (Monday). Whosoever knows this secret gets nine treasures of the Lord of Wealth (Kubera), and also health, wealth and prosperity.

After getting the Mantra he went a nearby village of his sister. The sister welcomed him and asked him the secret of his happiness. He told his sister and many other people of her village the secret Mantra of his happiness. The Brahman said the secret Mantra – is that Tuesday, Wednesday, Thursday, Friday, Saturday and Sunday are connected with other deities, and Lord Shiva is the deity of Monday. Whosoever fast and prays to Lord Shiva on Monday and knows this secret of week days will gets nine treasures of the Lord of Wealth (Kubera), and also good health, wealth and prosperity. As soon as the secret of Lord Shiva's fast on Monday was told to the Brahmin's sister, her house got filled with food and wealth. The Brahman was surprised to see the miracle of Mantra and getting richer due to the secret Mantra. Then he went to another friend's house. He repeated the same Mantra and his house also got filled with wealth. The Brahman went to his house and told his wife that she should not feel disappointed that he has come back empty handed. The Brahman told his wife that the Secret Mantra he has learnt from an ascetic is more valuable than wealth. As the Brahman told the Mantra to his wife, by the grace of Lord Shiva, his house got filled with food and wealth. The Brahman told his wife that we should give some of our food and wealth to the poor people and also marriages of poor girls to be arranged by us. After that the poor Brahmin lived very happily with his family.

Somvaar (Lord Shiva – the Deity of Monday) ki Katha – II

In the second story is mentioned that those who observe Monday fast, listen to this story in the afternoon and offer prayers to Lord Shiva would achieve success and prosperity.

pleasing to the gods. Most Hindus cultivate the plant in their houses, sometimes in a special brick enclosure called Vrindavan. It is watered and worshipped with the waving of lamps and circumambulation.

Tulsi plant has many medicinal qualities and that is why people treat it like a god. In the month of Kartik, women narrate stories about Tulsi. One of the stories about Tulsi is mentioned here. Once there was an old lady who would take her bath and water and pray before the plant of Tulsi. Tulsi wanted to help her to go to heaven after death, but she could not arrange it. Lord Krishna found Tulsi disturbed and wanted to help her. On the last day of Kartik the old lady worshipped Tulsi and died. Lord Krishna appeared and took the old lady to heaven on the request of Tulsi. Some people keep a fast in the memory of Tulsi in the middle of Kartik.

Tulsi's marriage

On an auspicious day between Kartik 11th to 15th (October-November), Lord Vishnu is every year married to Tulsi. Tulsi plant (Ocymum sanctum) was, in her former birth pious Vrinda, the daughter of Nemi. She got married to Jaladhar who was born from the sweat of Shiva, which he had thrown from his brow into the ocean. Jalladhar was born in Jala (water) therefore he was known Jaladhar (from water). As he was born in water he claimed back from Indra the fourteen treasures churned out of the ocean in the second incarnation of Vishnu. They were: goddess Lakshmi, Parijataka - flower tree, Sura - wine, Dhanvantri – heavenly physician, the Moon – nectar, Kamadhenu – cow of desires, Airavat – white elephant of the gods, Rambha – beautiful damsel, Kalakut – poison, Uchaisrava – seven headed horse of the chariot of the Sun god, the invincible missile of Vishnu, and the conch shell. Indra refused to give back these treasures and there was fight between Jaladhar and the gods.

Jaladhar's wife's virtue was so great that it endowed her husband divine power, so that even Shiva could not gain mastery over him. At last Vishnu changed himself in the form of her husband and seduced the faithful woman. Having lost something of his perfection through the infidelity of his wife, Jaladhar was easily slain by Shiva. She blamed Vishnu for deception and cursed him to become black stone (Salagram), and Vishnu cursed her to become Tulsi plant so that people can worship such a pious lady.

Salagram is a stone sacred and worshipped by the Hindus, because of its spirals are supposed to contain or to be typical of Vishnu. It is an ammonite found in the river Gandak, and is valued more or less highly according to the number of its spirals and perforations. According to the Atharva-veda the house without a Salagram is as impure as cemetery. The stone is usually kept wrapped in a nice cloth and is highly esteemed. It is believed that to touch the stone means absolution from all sins, and to be assured a place in heaven. Some people believe that the sacred Tulsi plant represent the hair of Vrinda and is believed to be occupied by her spirit every evening. In the morning she leaves the plant. Hindus grow Tulsi in the courtyard of their houses.

The Gadaki river in Nepal is revered as the occasional resting place for Vishnu, who visits it from time to time and lies in the riverbed embracing Vrinda (Tulsi shrub), which is found in the jungles nearby. But they have come to love each other so tenderly that they are married every year on the eleventh day of the month of Kartik. This ceremony marks the opening of the annual marriage season amongst Hindus. There are people who devoutly repeat this episode every year, in the hope that a place is surely reserved for them in heaven.

Vasant Panchami/Sri Panchami or Vasant

Vasant Panchami is a spring festival marking the first day of the spring season in the month of January-February. All the plants, trees, shrubs and plants are covered with flowers. Everyone gets up in the morning, takes bath and worship the sun, the earth and the Ganges. It is believed that on this day Lord Shiva burnt Kam (god of love) for disturbing him.

pleased with her devotion and restored her wealth and prosperity. Her lost husband also returned home and both of them kept Thursday fast regularly and lived a very happy family life.

Virvaar/Vrihaspati Vaar ki Katha – II (Banana Goddess – Lakshmi)

A poor young girl used to water a banana tree in her garden and play under it daily. One day she told her mother that she heard a strange voice from the tree. Her mother told her that banana goddess was pleased with her and she was hearing her voice. The girl heard the voice again and invited her to play with her. The Goddess came to play with her and gave her some money, sweets and fruits. The next day the Goddess was invited to the poor girl's house and was pleased with their devotion towards her. The Goddess told the girl to keep on watering the banana tree and she will appear before her in the form of a banana tree fruit. The Goddess offered them the gift of happiness and prosperity and vanished.

Virvaar/Vrihaspati Vaar ki Katha – III

In Puranas many stories are told about Lord Indra. Once he was sitting in the company of deities and Guru Vrihaspat*i appeared.* All the deities stood up to acknowledge his presence as a mark of respect, except Lord Indra. The Guru felt insulted by Lord Indra and left the place. Immediately Lord Indra realized his mistake and went to the Guru's hermit to apologize. But the Guru refused to see him.

A demon called Vrishwarsha took advantage of the situation and attacked and won the kingdom of Lord Indra. At the request of Indra, Brahma persuaded the Guru to pardon Indra for his mistake. The Guru agreed and blessed Indra to regain his kingdom back from the demon.

The moral of the story is that you will suffer if you are not respectful to your Guru.

2.

Ceremonies, rituals or sacraments

Ceremonies, rites and rituals

The whole body of scriptures dealing with the religious ceremonies and practices of Hindus is known as Kalpa-sutras (ritual texts).

The aims of the sacraments (rituals)

1. Removal of hostile influences. The main purpose is to remove hostile influences and attract beneficial ones, so that a human can grow and prosper without external hindrances and receive timely help and directions from gods. Most of the rituals have grown out of these beliefs. For removing the hostile influence it was considered essential to appease spirits and demons through praise, oblations and food, so that they may return satisfied with offerings, without causing injury to the individual. The householder wants to protect his family and regards it his duty to deal with them. The householder also invoked the help of gods and deities to drive away foul influences

2. Attraction of favourable influences to become a perfect human being and also to attain Moksha. The Hindus believe that every period of life is presided over by a deity. Usually the deity is invoked to confer boons and blessings on the man. At the time of conception Lord Vishnu is invoked, at the time of marriage Prajapati and at time of thread ceremony Brihaspati and so on. It is also believed that by touching things would also bring good luck and remove hostile influence. In the Simantonanyana (hair-parting) ceremonies a

branch of the fig tree is applied to the neck of the wife for fertility, good luck and prosperity. Stone treading ceremony - on which bride is asked to put her right foot and is told to be firm like a rock to protect her and groom's family honour. Touching the heart means bringing harmony between husband and wife or husband and wife. As the breath is a symbol of life, father is asked to breath thrice on the newly born child to strengthen its breaths.

3. The material gain of the rituals is to obtain progeny, long life, wealth, prosperity, strength and intellect. It is a firm belief that by offering prayers to god they will be rewarded in the form of animals, children, corn, food, a healthy body and intellect. By performing the sacraments of conception, birth, tonsure, and thread ceremony, seminal and uterine impurities are washed away. The rituals are calculated to remove the bodily defects transmitted from the parents, but they are not intended to remove the tint of sin arising from immoral parents. Another purpose of the rituals is the attainment of heaven and even Moksha or liberation from the cycle of birth and death. The rituals also enable one to attain the good qualities of the soul (mercy, tolerance, purity, calmness, right behaviour, charitable and freedom from greed and covetousness). The sacraments were a guide that directed the life of an individual to become a perfect human being; to make the body a valuable possession, a thing not to be discarded, but made holy, a thing to be sanctified, so that it might be a fitting instrument of the spiritual intelligence embodied in it.

Essential parts of sacraments (Samskaras)

1. Agni (Fire). The first and the most important part of the sacraments was Agni (Fire), which was always kindled in the beginning of every Samskara. The family hearth was the first holy of the holiest. By virtue of its usefulness, Fire assumed the role of the Lord of the house and also a messenger between gods and men. Agni (Fire) was believed to be a great protector against illness, demons and other hostile spirits. Therefore it was propitiated to ward off evil influences. It was an eternal witness during the thread and marriage ceremonies, for their ties may be valid and permanent. It was not the case with the Vedic Indians alone. The Greeks and Romans also made the hearth the centre of religious faith and rite

2. Prayers and blessings. Gods were prayed for the welfare of the family. In marriage "Seven steps ceremony" (Saptapadi) prayers are offered to Lord Vishnu for vital juice, prosperity, wealth, comfort, cattle and good friends etc. In the Upanayana (thread ceremony) prayers are offered for intellectual stimulation, purity, honesty and Brahamcharya during studentship. The most sacred Gayatri Mantra says: Let us meditate on the most excellent light of the creator (the Sun), may the sun guide our intellect. Prayers were offered for one's own good and blessings, and for welfare of our family and others. It was believed that blessings would transmit the good and influence the individual and people aimed at.

3. Sacrifice. It was believed that praise and prayer appeased gods, like men. Therefore they thought that gods also accepted gifts and presents like men. As some deities preside over a particular period of life, therefore they were invited, placated and feasted. Some other deities were also entertained as their spheres of influence were often overlapping.

4. Purifying with water. All the religions suggested that water was essential for a living being. That is why Hebrews called it "living water", and Christians use it in baptism (immersion in or sprinkling with water). In Islam ablution is essential before the prayers. In Hinduism sipping of water, sprinkling of water over persons and things became essential right from the beginning. The purifying effects of water were known after a bath in cool waters - he/she felt purified and refreshed. Many wells, springs, lakes, and rivers had miraculous healing property, so it was believed that some divine lived in each of them. The Hindus used water for removing contagious diseases, influence of evil spirits, and killing demons. Bath was to wash off physical, moral and spiritual impurities. Sipping of water in ceremonies symbolises washing off impurities or a symbolic bath. The Hindus led a life purified by water from conception to cremation and even after that. At the end of student career the youth was bathed, the bride and groom were bathed before nuptial ceremonies, and the dead were washed before cremation. Sipping many times in a day and sprinkling of water during rituals, for fame, glory, learning and good luck are prescribed by scriptures. The bride was sprinkled on her head for health, peace, prosperity and happiness.

5. Orientation. It was based on the picturesque symbolism of the path of the sun myths according to which different directions were ruled by different deities. It was believed that eastern direction was associated with light and warmth, life and happiness and glory; the west with darkness and cold, death and decay; south is the direction of Yama (god of death) as inauspicious. While making circumambulation in the rituals, the course of the sun was followed. During the funeral ceremonies the head of the dead was kept towards the south on the funeral pyre.

6. Symbolism. It was very important in Hindu sacraments. Stone was a symbol of strength and who mounted it was supposed to be invested with firmness in character. The student in Upanayana (thread) ceremony and the bride in marriage ceremonies were required to step on a stone signifying their firmness in devotion to the teacher and the husband. Sesamum and rice were symbols of fertility and prosperity. Anointment was symbol of love and affection, eating together was a symbol of union, touching the hearts means joining hearts, grasping the hand means taking full responsibility, looking towards the sun symbolises brilliance and lustre etc.

7. Taboos (forbidden things). Life was the central mystery of the world for an early man. There were so many forbidden things during early pregnancy. It was felt necessary to take precautions against dangers. There were things connected with lucky and unlucky days, months and years. Unfavourable incidents, economic and astronomical, and happenings like death, disease and defeat presumed some days, months and years as unlucky. There were also taboos based on rational grounds. During natural calamity, political revolution, death of a person, menses etc., and rituals were postponed. A particular food was allowed in a particular sacrament. Fasting was also sometimes meant for producing ecstasy.

8. Magic. Magical elements were also sometimes found in the sacraments. Magic was performed for safe and easy delivery, for warding off evil spirits etc. But later the Brahmanical law books declared magic as a sin. . The magicians were classed with rogues and scoundrels and the king was asked to punish them.

9. Divination – predictions. Of all divinatory methods astrology played the greatest role in rituals. Detailed astrological predictions are prescribed in books for rituals to be performed under an auspicious planet. The Linga Purana has completely dealt with this subject.

10. Social customs. In addition to the above religious beliefs, rites and ceremonies, the sacraments contain social customs and usages and rules about race improvement, ethics, hygiene, medicine etc. Marriage settlements were made according to social customs and rules. In selection of bride and groom, in copulation, pregnancy and rearing of children the rules of eugenics and social purity were followed. The life of a student, householder was regulated according to the moral laws of the time. Life was protected from demons, disease and accidents by prescribing rules of health, diet and medicine. Rules of sanitation were observed in then house, during menses, confinement, and death in a family and other occasions in life.

11. Common sense elements. These elements were connected with religious ideas. The whole sacramental atmosphere was fragrant with spiritual significance. Under the sacramental canopy the recipient felt exalted, elevated and sanctified. During marriage everyone felt happy decorating the house with sprouts, leaves, flowers etc., and dressing the bride and groom with fitting costumes and ornaments according to their social status. The programme of music was to echo the general happiness and to entertain the guests. The Varaha Grihasutra made the instrumental music as a regular constituent of marriage ceremonies.

Pre-natal sacraments

Garbhadaan (conception)

The rite of making a woman pregnant by her husband was called Garbhdaan. There are many references in the Vedic hymns explaining - how to approach a woman for conception. There are many prayers in the Vedic hymns pointing to the description of actual copulation and conception. The proper time for conception was from the fourth to the sixteenth night after the monthly course of the wife. It was believed that fourth night was ceremoniously pure for conception. Only nights were prescribed for conception and daytime was prohibited. The husband approached his wife every month when she was pure after her menses to go to bed with him for conception, prayed to gods for placing the embryo into her womb and then finished fertilisation. It is believed that some kind of ceremony was performed on this occasion. According to literature available, the husband embraced his wife and conception proper took place with prayers to god and an indication to scattering semen. The husband then touched the heart of his wife, reclining over her right shoulder with the verse that we should have many children. It was also felt that the duty of wife approaching the husband was equally binding when she became pure after her menses. A woman who does not approach and go to her husband would become a swine in her next life.

In the Vedic literature we get references where a widow invites her brother-in-law to raise children for her husband. Manu and many other Smrities (oral traditions) allow the widow or the wife of an impotent or invalid person to bear children from the brother of her husband or a Brahman.

Pumsavana (ritual for the birth of a male child)

After the establishment of a pregnancy a ritual of Pumsavana was performed for the birth of a male child. It consists of many prayers to God and a medicinal herb to the pregnant woman for the birth of a male child. The hymn expressed the wish that a handsome male child should be born. Some kind of celebration was made with prayers for the birth of a son. Some sort of medicinal herb was also given to the pregnant woman with the hymn, "the plants of which heaven has been the father, earth the mother, ocean the root, let those herbs of the gods favour her, in order to acquire a son." During the Grihyasutra period the Banyan tree juice was inserted into the right nostril of the woman with hymns conducive to the birth of a son. The rite was usually performed before the foetus begins to move in the womb. It should be performed when the moon was on a male constellation. This time was regarded as favourable for producing a male child. Inserting the juice of the Banyan tree was a device meant for preventing abortion and ensuring the birth of a male child. It is believed that the Banyan tree has got the properties of removing all kinds of troubles during pregnancy. The hymn usually expressed the wish for a handsome and healthy child.

Svah or Bhur bhuvah svah (I put into your mouth everything good for your intellect and well being).

Ayush

The next ceremony was the *Ayusha* or the rite for ensuring a long life for the child.

Strength

The father next performed another rite for the strength, martial, healthy and pure life of the child. When the ceremonies were over, presents were offered to the priest and gifts and alms distributed.

3.

Namakarna (Name-giving)

Ever since men evolved a language, they have tried to give names to things of daily use in their life. With the progress of social consciousness, men were also named, because without particular names of individuals it was impossible to carry on the business of a cultured society. The adoption of a second name is assumed for success and distinction in life. Usually people have two names; one was the popular one, and the other being a patronymic or matronymic. It is believed that one who is desirous of fame, his name should consist of two syllables, one who desires holy lustre, and his name should contain four syllables. For boys even number of syllables were prescribed and for girls uneven number of syllables.

According to Hindu mythology, everything in the world is a manifestation of God; therefore the name of any entity can be used as a given name. A name is the primary means of social intercourse. It brings realisation, merits and is also considered as the root of good fortune.

We are here concerned with ceremonial naming of persons only, but I have given here a brief description of Hind names. It is a vast subject that would really need a lot of space to give it justice. It is a big subject both in time and quantity. In time and quantity - because our earliest text (Rig Veda) is dated about 10,000 BC, and for all of the 1652 or so languages of India the names are usually taken from Sanskrit sources. Throughout the Vedic period the name given to a person was his own secular name and one or more other names derived from a variety of sources including either

Nishkramana (first outing)

Every step in the life of the child was a celebration for the parents and the family, and it was celebrated with appropriate religious ceremonies. Usually forty days after the birth of the child or on the fourth month after the birth, the child was taken out of the house and introduced to the outer world. Therefore, the protection of the child from evil eye, gods were worshipped for the health, development and well being of the child. Usually the parents took the child out of the house in the courtyard and make the child look at the sun and sky and prayed that all the gods led by Indra protect the child. The child was brought back to the family deity in the house and the deity was worshipped with instrumental music. The guardians of eight directions, the sun, the moon, Vasudev and sky were also propitiated. The child was also taken to the temple for blessings.

Annaprashana (first feeding)

Feeding the child with solid food was the next important stage in the life of the child. While the quantity of the mother's milk diminished the child required solid food. This ceremony was connected with the physical need of the child at six or seven months. Food being a life giving substance, it was thought that there was something mysterious about it from which life emanated. The source of energy was to be infused into the child with the help of gods. Praise of food is found in the Vedas and the Upanishads and they were sung at ordinary dinner and during the first feeding of the child. The food of different kinds and flavours should be mixed together and given to the child to eat. The food was cooked with appropriate Vedic verses. The prayer was offered that all the senses of the child should be gratified so that he/she may live a happy and contended life. The ceremony signifies a timely reminder for the good health of mother and child.

Karnavedha (boring the ears)

Boring of different limbs for wearing ornaments is current among wild tribes all over the world. Boring of ears in Vedic times was ornamental in its origin, but later some ancient doctors suggested that it was useful for preventing Hernia and some other diseases. It was recommended that ears of every child should be bored for protection, and it became a part of religious ceremony so that the chances of some diseases may be minimised. This ceremony was usually performed on the eighth or the twelfth month after the birth of the child. The idea of boring at early age was that it would be easier and less troublesome to the child. Usually a surgeon pierced the ears, but a goldsmith who made the needle was also given the privilege of piercing the ears. Gold, silver and iron needles were used in piercing ears. The right ear of the boy and the left of the girl was bored first. After boring oil should be applied to the ears. In the end presents were exchanged and guests and priest entertained.

Chaudakarna or Mundan ceremony (tonsure)

Cutting the hair was essential to keep head clean. According to medical book (Sushruta) shaving and cutting the hair and nails remove impurities and give delight, freshness, prosperity and happiness, strength and beauty to the body. At the basis of tonsure ceremony the idea of health and beauty was prominent. No doubt, at present, the tonsure (Mundan) ceremony is performed at the temple, but so is some other rites e.g., the Upanyana. In olden days the ceremonies of those children were performed at the temple who were born after a long disappointment. In scriptures, there is not an innate connection between the tonsure ceremony and its dedication to a deity. The ceremony is found in Vedic period and also in Sutra period. In olden days the ceremony used to take place at the end of the first, third year, fifth or seventh

ceremony he becomes dvija (twice-born), and is admitted to the privileges of his society and has access to the sacred books. The sacred thread is usually worn over the left shoulder, going diagonally across the breast, and under the right arm to the right hip. There are three threads in Janeo remind a young man of the Pranava (OM, the symbol of Absolute) Medha (intelligence) and Shradha (diligence), the three essential guides for education and the life of a householder. He is taught the most sacred Gayatri Mantra (hymn) or the worship of the Sun so that he may absorb its brilliance and effulgence.

In ancient India girls were admitted to the Upanayana ceremony at the age of eight. Fundamentally the ceremony was a sacrament symbolising the boy's readiness for receiving sacred knowledge. Several related observances were incorporated into the regular ceremony. Before the ceremony the mother and son ate together for the last time. It marked the end of an irregular life of a child and reminded the boy that he was no longer an irresponsible child. After this Upanayana the mother could no more take food with him as he was going to be away from home for receiving education and getting married afterwards. The following fifteen steps marked the completion of the ceremony:

i. The youth, wearing loincloth was brought before the Guru for initiation, thus giving the name Upanayana, to the whole ceremony.

ii. The father requests the Guru to accept the boy as a student.

iii. The Guru in turn hands the boy over to the care of the Gods Savitri, Pushan, Ashvins, Somna, Agni and Prajapati.

iv. The Guru asks the name of the boy and other particulars.

v. The Guru accepts him as student and touches his shoulder as a token of acceptance.

vi. The Guru gives him clothes to wear.

vii. The Guru ties around the waist of the boy a girdle made of a triple cord of cotton for purity in thought, word and deed. It was from this the sacred thread (Janeo) evolved.

viii. The Guru gives him a staff (danda) symbolising the beginning of his long journey to perfection in education and all other aspects of a civilised human being.

ix. The Guru fills his cupped hands with water and empties them into the cupped hands of his pupil with blessings of success and happiness.

x. The Guru commands the student to mount a stone and ask him to be as firm as stone.

xi. A student is given to eat curds and clear his mind to grasp and follow all the instructions of the Guru.

xii. The student is shown the sun and told that the light of the sun should be his ideal in his quest for knowledge.

xiii. Gayatri mantra is taught to the student and he learns the method of recitation.

xiv. The student is taught how to place a sacrificial wood into the fire with hymns.

xv. The ceremony concludes when the student walks around the sacred fire.

Sacred thread ceremony is also performed by holy men as a condition for initiation into their order. Those who have received the sacred thread renew it after performing certain ceremonies on the Shravan (full moon).

Samavartana of Snana (end of studentship)

Samavartana means returning from the house of the Guru (teacher). This ceremony marked the end of student life, and the beginning of Grihastha (householder, married man living with his wife and family). The education usually finished at the age of twenty-four and this ceremony was more or less a license for marriage after that age. At present the ceremony is performed either with the Upanayana or the Vivah (marriage) and the only remnants of the procedure are the ceremonial bath and the decoration of the person with Vedic hymns. It was considered that for the comfortable life of a householder it required a cooling influence, which was symbolised by bathing and indicated by the Vedic hymns associated with it.

The marriage and other Samskaras (sacraments) are expressions of human beliefs, sentiments, hopes and weaknesses, and they are useful for human needs. With the progress of science many natural forces are not feared in modern times as they used to be in olden days. The magic hold of religion in some fields of life is loosened, but religious sanction is still required to sanctify the ceremonies. Inspite of progress in science and technology the man is still experiencing the mystic touch of the invisible God for the source of life. These mysteries of God are keeping alive the religious sentiments in man.

4.

Marriage Ceremonies

Importance of Marriage

According to Hindus, marriage (Vivaha) is one of the major Samskaras (sacraments) of life. It is binding not only in this life but also in the next life. It is a union of not only the bride and groom, but also their families. According to tradition the sage Svetaketu, son of Uddalaka, stopped the once universally prevalent custom of indiscriminate sexual union. Sage Svetaketu (meaning white light) established the system of one man and one wife about 7,000 BC. In this way the Hinduism had contributed a lot to the world by bringing marriage back to its legitimate state. It had contributed more by that alone to the general peace, happiness, stability, and civilisation of human race, than it would have been possible for it to do in any other department of divine providence.

Polygamy was tolerated amongst persons of high rank, such as kings, princes, statesmen, and others. Anyway, this plurality of wives amongst the great is looked upon as a violation of natural law and custom, in fact, as an abuse. The Hindu gods had only one wife each. Brahma had only Saraswati; Vishnu, Lakshmi; Shiva, Parvati; Ram, Sita; and Krishna, Rukamani. This proves that from the earliest times the Hindus looked upon marriage as a legal union between two persons of opposite sex. The unnatural custom of polygamy, which finds a place amongst some nations, may be attributed to sinful lust, to abuse the power of the strong over the weak, and to the dominion of one sex over the other. It is evidently contrary to the intention of the creator, who, when He created the father of mankind, gave him only one woman as wife, and indeed ordained that man and his one wife should form as one unit.

Manu (sage & lawgiver, 600 BC) stated that Hindu marriage (one man and one wife) was for all-time, irrevocable, and indissoluble. This is the Vedic wedding, and started thousands of years ago during the Vedic times. Customs and ceremonies of marriage differ from region to region and even from village to village, but Sanskrit hymns chanted in marriage ceremonies are the same in all the parts of India.

In India, amongst its various castes and tribes of Hindus, forms of marriage are to be seen from the simplest modes of mutual consent to many other forms of marriage. In many parts of India, there are also marriage customs, forbidding and encouraging Hindus to marry within and outside the caste, sect, tribe and race. Marriage received great importance even in early times. It was not only a social necessity, but also a religious duty for every individual. It is considered that a man is incomplete without a wife. Man without a wife is half man, and the second half is wife. In Hinduism marriage is the most important and most engrossing event of life. It is a subject of endless conversation and of the most prolonged preparations. Although marriage is considered natural for every one, but those who wish to remain unmarried, for pious reasons, are given great respect by the society. It is only for those persons who have renounced the world, and have chosen to lead a life of contemplation, who can take vows of celibacy. In any other case marriage is the rule, and every one is under the obligation of discharging the great debt to his ancestors, namely, that of begetting a son. The Sanskrit word for son is putra, means literally, one who saves from put or hell – the hell into which parents without son falls. At present the proportion of sexes is not equal in all parts of India, but still one rarely meets a woman/man who is not, or has not been married. Blind, dumb, deaf, or lame, except diseased, all find husbands/wives amongst Hindus, whose low fortunes or low position do not allow them to aspire to an alliance with more attractive partner.

Other people also held marriage in high esteem. Among the people of Israel it was respected for the same reason as among the Hindus. During the age of Messianic prophecies, marriage gained an added sanctity from the precious possibility that the fruit of the union might be a promised messiah of the Jews, its long desired saviour from oppression. In Greece marriage was also highly respected sacred ceremony. Celibacy was regarded as a serious offence, a crime against the household gods. Romans also regarded marriage as a sacred act and celibacy with public disapproval. In Christianity marriage is a spiritual and physical union and latter is impossible without the former.

The Origin of Marriage

Marriage attracted much attention of the people and various ceremonies gathered round it. A popular theory is that marriage sprang from the family, which developed into the clan. Among the tribal people – only very slowly developed the idea of kinship, the primary one being that as they held their women in common they were never certain of relationship, except through the mother's side. The source of marriage is in the utter helplessness of the newborn - as he/she needs both the mother and father for protection and food during a varying period of time. It means that marriage has its source in the family, rather than the family in marriage, and the various roots of the permanent union of sexes are found in parental duties. It was natural for a woman to expect sufficient protection during the critical period of her confinement and also adequate protection of her child in its helpless state of infancy that made her to find a husband in life. The lovemaking and other means of enticement helped in securing the union. The desire for a son, the protection of

were considered to be grown up by the time of their marriage. The rules were the same in the Indian subcontinent and Sri Lanka and amongst the Buddhist population. The custom of marrying daughters in the order of their age was also well established. It means that the eldest daughter should be married first.

Dharmashastra (jurisprudence) lowered the marriageable age of the bride, and stated that a girl should be married before she attains womanhood. The reasons for the introduction of the practice of child-marriage cannot be definitely assigned. There is a reference in the Dharmasastra (or laws of Manu) about Greeks, Scythians and Persians, as being a bad influence that they brought the gradual decline in the status of women and the growing assertion of authority by men over women and children. Foreign invasions of India began in the third or the fourth century BC . The Greeks, the Bactrian, the Parthians and the Scynthians, who were less civilised than the Indians, occupied the Northwest provinces of India. The position of women was very low amongst these peoples and was regarded as an article of enjoyment. The social life of the Hindus was greatly influenced by these foreigners. Perhaps for the safety of girls from foreigners, child marriage became fashionable. The marriage of children and the performance of betrothal by their parents were not unknown at one time even in European countries. The legal age of marriage in England was only 14 for boys and 12 for girls, until it was raised to 16 for both in 1929.

Widow re-Marriage

The re-marriage of a widow was strongly reprobated by Manu as being improper. It is interesting to note that in the Arthasastra of Kautilya (300 BC) the re-marriage of widows was highly appreciated. Later Smriti writers like Narada took a more generous view and recognised the right of a widows to marry a second husband. Some times a widow was allowed to marry with the husband's brother and other relatives if the brother was not available. While it is probable that the vast majority of women preferred a married life, some of them, either by choice or by necessity, led a life of celibacy.

There was a time when owing to the growing ascendancy of the ascetic ideal life for widows the practice of re-marriage fell into disrepute. Asceticism has been practiced in India as a method of discipline and self-restraint, and the ascetic ideal has never been exalted at the expense of the ideal of the householder. Nearly all the Rishis (seers) were married men and their wives equally with them were looked upon as exemplars of the highest virtue. The fact that anthropomorphic conceptions of the deity in India included both the female and the male elements is an illustration of the absence in the Hindu mind of all notions of impurity about sex. Hinduism never attached any notion of impurity to sex. Marriage was regarded not as a concession to the weakness of human nature, nor was married life regarded as a morally inferior condition to virginity. The position of women during Vedic times was much superior to women in later times.

Inter-caste Marriage

The marriage in the clan (gotra = same family name or from same ancestor) was not allowed. Marriage among maternal or paternal cousin was strictly prohibited. Marriage within the father's or the mother's family was considered not conducive to good health.

The Reddi of the South India are divided into 24 clans, who marry in their own clans. They profess to be Vaishnava (worshipper of Vishnu). As a law, the men marry their sister's daughter, but an aunt does not marry her nephew. Property descends through the issue of a son and granddaughter, uncle and niece. If a man refuses to marry his own sister's daughter, his father's property descends not to him, but to the man who marries the rejected woman.

With the Maravar of Ramnad and Sivaganga disparity of ages is not considered. Some of their subdivisions do not marry into the father's family, but Hindus in South India generally intermarry with the mother's relations. Marriage of

Traditionally marriage proposals were sent by the people of the bridegroom for the hand of the bride. The Rigveda suggests that in the marriage of Soma and Surya the proposal was sent to Surya, through two Ashvins, by the father of the bride. This was the ideal pattern of Hindu marriage described in the Vivah Sutra. The marriage took place when the former accepted the proposal agreeing to give away his daughter in marriage. The Sutras (domestic rituals – 6BC) also describe the same practice.

One Sutra has described this ceremony in detail. The bridegroom's party reached the girl's house carrying with them flowers, fruits, barley and a pot of water. They disclosed their identity, asked for the hand of the girl in marriage. After the parties expressed their willingness, the bridegroom's party performed some rituals as suggested by the priest of the bride's family. The deal was considered as being confirmed. The practice seems to have continued even in the times of Kalidasa (300 AD) and Bana Bhatta. Kalidasa in his Kumarsambhavam says that Himavata, the father of Parvati, had not agreed to give his daughter to Sankara who was Ayachita (one who had not made a demand) for the hand of his daughter. According to Bana Bhatta's Harishchandra, Prince Grahavarma sent his messengers for the marriage of Rajyashri, the sister of Harsha.

During the medieval times, the custom of the bridegroom approaching the bride's father was dropped, and instead his father went to bride's house with some friends on behalf of his son. The custom is still used in the Deccan and other parts of South India in the form of formally seeing the girl and settling the marriage.

In the later period, however, the practice entirely changed and instead of the boy's parents initiating the marriage proposal, this was replaced by the girl's parents. In northern and some other parts of India, the custom has been reversed. The brother and father of the bride, a Brahman, a few friends and relations would go to the bridegroom's house and offer him fruits, sweets, flowers, clothes, and some money to settle the betrothal. This custom is known as Tilaka, and is very popular in northern India. In the opinion of some authorities this ceremony should take place one day before the marriage, but usually it takes place many days before the marriage day. After the betrothal, an auspicious day is fixed for the wedding ceremonies. In some families astrologers are consulted and they are very particular about fixing the proper time for all the marriage ceremonies. Consequently, the ceremony came to be performed at the house of the boy, in the same way as the rituals of the Tilak (auspicious mark on forehead) ceremony prevalent in the present times. In return, the groom's parents perform some rituals by giving gifts to the bride at her home.

Music in Marriage ceremonies

It is mentioned in the Vedas that dance and music are arts associated with worship and ritual, and therefore it is clothed in sanctity. Women of the royal families took dancing as an accomplishment and a cultural asset, and they studied the art very seriously.

Indian music is a relic of the world's oldest music. It has much in common with the musical systems of the Chinese, the Egyptians, Assyrians and Arabs. In Indian music, musical sound is called nada, and nada is called Brahman or Divine Reality itself. Music is at the heart and soul of Hindu/Sikh and Muslim marriages. A week before the marriage ceremony, ladies Sangeet (music party) takes place every day in the evening at both the bride and groom's houses.

Background music of Shehnai and flute are regarded as auspicious for wedding ceremonies. The flute and lute (Vina) players, and the ritual singers, thus, played a very important part in the rituals. The employment of music was not only for gaiety; it had an emotional basis, and worked as a magic

hold brass trays, and forming into a circle, move forwards and backwards with little slow steps, singing in chorus.

In Kulu (Himachal Pradesh) the men wear their traditional tight trousers and tunics with bright coloured shawls and caps. They form into a circle, and holding a handkerchief in their right hands, they wave it with supple wrists and move round and round in a stepping of eight beats. Then suddenly two or three dancers come into the centre commence dancing with swords. The dance is accompanied with Dholak, trumpets and small clarinets. Musicians sing in praise of deities and recall the old days of chivalry and romance.

Rouf

Women in Jammu do the Rouf dance on festive occasions. The dancers form two rows of ten girls each, and place their arms across one another's back - moving forward and backward. The dancers sing together, and each row of girls takes up the refrain as the other starts the line. They all dress in bright coloured skirts and draperies, with many ornaments, for the dance to look attractive.

Dandiya Ras

In Gujarat Dandiya Ras dance is very popular, and twenty-four men who hold short lacquered sticks do it. The song accompanying it tells of one of the important episodes from the epic poem the Ramayana, embracing the banishment of Prince Rama, the abduction of Sita, the war against Ravana and the victorious return home to Ayodhya of Ram and Sita. Singing in chorus, the dancers form an intricate series of movements, first with rhythmic six-step, holding hands and moving round in a circle. Then increasing the speed they beat their sticks and each dancer swiftly spins on their tip-toes. After this, they beat one another's sticks, and wave them with over and over; change places and moves in a complete circle, and finally, form into an inner and outer circle. The speed of dance increases in which the outer circle of dancers bend and cross their sticks and then the inner circle of dancers cross their sticks above their heads. Finally, the dancers form a bridge with their sticks in twos, moving opposite to one another, while every alternate man dances between, making a running circle with moving bridges. They squat, turn, and then run in the opposite direction. As the dance increases in speed, the dancers form various patterns and sit down in-groups to take some rest. The dance is very vigorous, and the tune of the drumbeats enhances the poetic metre of the songs.

Garba dance

The Garba dance is very popular on festive occasions and during the Dusehra festival. The dancers go round and round in circles, bending to the right and left and forward, stamping the feet in a rhythm of four counts, and clapping their hands in sweeping gestures. The themes of the dance are from the life of Krishna, depicting social life of the village and romances. A singer leads the first line and the rest follow in chorus.

Aims of Marriage

There are four aims of a Hindu marriage, Dharma, Praja, Artha and Kama. Of these Dharma occupies the highest place, Praja the second and Artha/Kama is regarded as the last.

Dharma signifies a righteous act or the good code of conduct of the bride and groom, an individual or group; the precepts of social behaviour, as found in the Dharma-sastra (law scriptures); the practice of virtues enjoined by ethics, leading to proper behaviour and moral conduct. The general meaning " that which is right" — implies justice, virtue, morality, good conduct, good communication, integrity, honesty and righteousness etc. Acts of charity, austerity or sacrifice are also included in Dharma. Shankaraacharya (learned teacher 758 AD) considered Dharma as a virtuous path characterised by rites and duties as revealed by the Vedas; it is a direct means to the secular and spiritual welfare of living beings. Honesty, proper communication and integrity between husband and wife are also an essential part of Dharma.

Praja means procreation; it is regarded as the second aim of marriage. The debt towards their ancestors was considered to have been discharged by procreation (continuing the family). Its importance is rooted in the Rigveda, and is shown through the large number of prayers, which are found through out the marriage ceremony.

Artha and Kama should be enjoyed in married life. Artha is said to refer to all the proper means necessary for acquiring worldly prosperity, such as wealth or power. And Kama refers to all the desires in man for the enjoyment and satisfaction of the life of the senses. Kama refers to the totality of the invested desires and drives of man, including learning to co-operate, understanding one another and builds tolerance for a happy married life.

In Hinduism woman is held in high regard and is believed that if the women of the family are respected and kept happy, the family attains prosperity and good luck.

The ceremony of choosing and talking to each other takes place, when a willing boy and a girl meet and their parents talk about marriage arrangements. Usually an astrologer, by this time has been consulted about the auspicious date of betrothal and marriage. The astrologer is also asked whether or not the stars offer any insurmountable obstacle to the union.

Marriage ceremonies in various parts of India

Customs and ceremonies of marriage differ from region to region and even from village to village. Since customs play a very significant role in determining the code of conduct and religious and ritual performance of the Hindus, the Sutras suggest that one should learn about the requisite customs and ceremonies from the old women of the village. For centuries these customs have played a significant part in the performance of rituals. They have been classified into three types, namely, the caste customs, the family customs and the local customs. Whereas the Vedic ceremonies are performed with the recital of Mantras as described in the sacred texts of the Hindus, there are various other ceremonies, which are based on various types of customs, differing from caste to caste and region to region. The Grihyasutras may be treated as marriage manuals since they mainly describe the entire performance of the sacrament. However, as they belong to different schools of the Vedas and were composed at different times, the nature and sequence of the ceremonies show great divergence. There seems to be a lack of unanimity regarding the number of ceremonies and the order in which they have to be performed.

However, the whole process of the marriage ceremony may be regarded as composed of three successive stages, preliminary rituals commencing from the end of studentship; marriage proper and succeeding rituals. The ceremonies prescribed in marriage proper may again be divided into two parts, the principal ceremonies and the subsidiary rituals. Usually ceremonies start after the selection of bride and groom. In the beginning, they were simple, but as marriage was a very important and festive occasion in the communal life, all sorts of merry making and amusements were associated with it in the form of music, dance and feasts etc. Decoration of the house and adornment of the bride and bridegroom expressed aesthetic motives natural to any important event in social life. A large group of ceremonies symbolises the union between the husband and wife, e.g. joining of hands, tying of garments, touching of hearts etc.

Many ceremonies are performed to ward of evil influences connected with the event. The gods are worshipped for boons and blessings.

A few days before the wedding, the ceremony of Mridaharana (bringing some earth or clay) ceremony is performed. On the ninth or seventh day before the marriage, in an auspicious moment with music and dancing, one should go to the northern or eastern direction of his house to fetch the earth for growing sprouts in a pot of clay. The ceremonies proceeding the marriage day are the following: First, the most auspicious God Ganesha is worshipped and his symbol is installed in the nuptial canopy. Another ceremony performed before marriage is besmearing the bride and the bridegroom with ointment of turmeric root and oil, a day before the wedding. The substance not is only useful to the body, but also auspicious.

It is mentioned in Atharvaveda that at wedding the bride wore beautiful robe, headdress and jewellery. Her treasure-chest containing her dowry was placed in her chariot. On the day of marriage she was bathed in water consecrated with Vedic verses. The bride was made to stand on a stone, to represent the lap of the earth. The bridegroom took her hand muttering appropriate verses and promised to cherish her. Then the bridegroom presented to her robes and jewels with which she was invested. After saying some prayers to drive away evil influences, they started on a marriage procession in a chariot to bridegroom's house. Groom and bride after reaching the house they sat next to each other before the household fire, and worshipped Agni (fire). They get blessings from every one present and pray that the presence of the bride proves beneficial to all the family. Consummation of the marriage immediately followed the nuptial ceremony.

The main outlines of Hindu marriage today are the same in all the parts of India. They are also the same what they were during the Vedic times, except some local and tribal differences - in details and arrangement of hymns. Usually local customs prevalent in one's own province and village are followed, after consulting old men and women, in some marriages.

Vivah (marriage) – definition

According to Hindus, marriage (Vivaha) is one of the major Samskaras (sacraments) of life. It is binding not only in this life but also in the next life. It is a union of not only the bride and groom, but also their families. Sage Svetaketu (meaning white light) established the system of one man and one wife about 7,000 BC. Manu (sage & lawgiver, 600 BC) stated that Hindu marriage was for all-time, irrevocable, and indissoluble. This is the Vedic wedding, and started thousands of years ago during the Vedic times.

In the olden days, a Hindu wedding lasted for about four to five days, but in modern times the ceremony is completed in one day. Usually a priest will chant the Sanskrit mantras (hymns) and the bride and groom, and most of the guests do not understand the meaning of ceremonies. A priest who can explain the meaning of ceremonies in a regional language or Hindi and English will be in great demand in future.

Forms of Marriage in Ancient India

There are eight forms of marriage referred to by Manu Smriti and other ancient lawgivers: Brahma, Daiva, Arsha, Prajapatya, Asura, Gandharva, Rakshasa and Paishacha.

(i) Brahma. The purest and the most evolved method of marriage was Brahma type. In this type of marriage the girl was given by her father with such ornaments as he could afford, to a man of character and learning, whom he invited voluntarily and received respectfully without taking any thing in return. It is evident from the above that many forms of marriage were practiced among the Hindus before the rule of marriage established by the sage Svetaketu.The Hindus perform now-a-days Brahma (Brahman-like) marriage. It is based on the mutual love and affection of the families. It is the gift of a daughter, or giving away your daughter to her bridegroom. It forms the basis of proper Hindu marriage, arranged/approved by the parents and attended by religious ceremonies. It is free from coercion and greed, but suitable financial help to bride and bridegroom is in some cases/ families obligatory.

(ii) Daiva. In this form the father gave the girl away to a priest, who officiated at a sacrifice commenced by him. According to Baudhayana, the girl was given as a Dakshina (sacrificial fee). Priests very often received from their princely patrons, noble maidens or slave girls for services at sacrifices who were called Vadhus.

(iii) Arsha. According to this method the father of the bride married her to a Rishi for his vast knowledge and spiritual culture.

(iv) Prajapatya. According to this system, the father gave his daughter to a suitor to the distinct understanding that they should both perform their civic and religious duties together. This type of marriage happened in a free society where there was no seclusion of women, and an adult groom came forward to ask the hand of an adult bride. There was no child marriage in this custom.

(v) Asura (undivine) marriage. According to this form a bridegroom receives a grown up maiden after having given, according to his own will, as much wealth as he can afford to the kinsmen and the bride herself, and she accepts it without any pressure from outside. It implies a sort of elopement and money is paid in settlement of the anger of the bride's people and the security of the bride herself. It may be illustrated by the marriage of Pandu and Madri of the Mahabharata. Manu Smriti condemns this sort of marriage where the bride is sold.

The similar custom of dowry to be offered by the father of the bride to the bridegroom is not to be found in Vedic or later times. In the Aitareya Brahmana a dowry marriage is called Pashuvivah (animal marriage). At the time of the child marriage system the dowry came into existence as the father became anxious to marry his child daughter within a limited time. At present, it is felt that the demand of dowry is a great impediment in the selection of a proper bride or bridegroom, and both the law and public opinion is against dowry. In India the giving and accepting of dowry is punishable by law.

In England during Saxon times the father would sell his daughter, as the women were very valuable as labourers, and the father was to be compensated for his loss. However, after the Crusades there were more women than men, so now the father gives his daughter away.

(vi) Gandharva – is the love or romantic form of marriage. In this marriage a bride and groom arrange among themselves out of their attraction towards each other. Many authorities praised it as it was produced from much attraction and love. The marriage of Shakuntala and Dushyanta may be cited as an illustration.

(vii) Rakshasa (demon) marriage: according to Manu – the capture of a girl by force while she is crying and weeping, having killed her relatives. This method was prevalent in ancient warring tribes and the captive women were enjoyed as war booties. The capture of a girl without her wishes (Rakshasa marriage) was not allowed during the Vedic period.

(viii) Paishacha. The least approved method was Paishacha (carrying off a girl who was sleepy, intoxicated, or unconscious). Manu defines as being 'when a man cohabits with a girl in loneliness when she is sleepy, mad or intoxicated, it is called Paishacha method'. The union of Usha and Pradyumna may be cited as an illustration. During Vedic and ancient times this type of marriage was considered unlawful.

Some other forms of Marriage

Marriage by exchange. Some poor parents, whose children do not attract the notice of matchmakers, arrange the marriage of their sons and daughters by exchange. It is not a voluntary custom, but a practice forced by circumstances.

Popular forms of Marriage

At present the only two methods of marriage in use are the Brahma and the Asura. In the first the girl is given away to a person without accepting anything from him. In the second, the father accepts money from the bridegroom, as the price of his daughter. The modern system of fixing dowry, in some families, and to make it the main consideration in settling the marriage does not existed in the ancient times.

Auspicious - Marriage Day

According to ancient Hindu books, marriage is to be celebrated at an auspicious time. According to Paraskara and Sankhyayana, it should be celebrated during the period when the sun is northerly. Nakshatyra and Paksha are also important considerations for the settlement of time. Paraskara holds that under the constellations Uttaraphalguni, Uttarshadha and Uttarabhadrapada and the two constellations following each of them, or under Svati, Mrigasira or Rohini marriage can be solemnised. Asvalayana Sutra (work on domestic rituals) points out that during the ascendant phase of the moon (second half of the month) marriages and other auspicious ceremonies should be performed. Hiranyakeshin prescribes five periods of time for performing the marriage ceremony, namely morning, forenoon, midday, afternoon and evening. The astrologicals were very particular about fixing the proper time for every detail of the marriage ceremony. In the morning of the marriage day, the bride and groom, at their respective homes, take the nuptial bath with scented water and recital of Vedic verses indicative of the physical union of the bride and groom.

Marriage hymns and ceremonies

The ceremonies and its order differ from region to region and even from village to village, but the Mantras (hymns) from the Vedas are the same. Grihya Sutras (rules for religious rituals in the home) may be taken as a marriage manual, but since they were composed at different times, the present day wedding service is based on three priestly manuals. The Mantras (hymns) are taken from Puranas (old religious literature), the Rig Veda, the Yajur-veda, Mantra-Brahmana, Aitareya-Brahmana, and Grihya Sutras of Asvalayana, Hiranyakeshi and Bauddhayana. The Asvalayana Grihya Sutra gives the order of rituals.

The marriage service can last anywhere between one and half-hour to four hours, and the bride and groom are asked to repeat Sanskrit mantras after the priest in certain rituals. The religious rituals with Sanskrit mantras provide a cultural continuity. The ceremony also gives an opportunity to many guests especially women to show off their colourful expensive Saris (red-white, yellow, and green), dresses and jewellery, reflecting their material wealth and success.

Significance of ceremonies

Constancy, faithfulness, self-control, love, self-abnegation are the virtues, which can be best developed during married life. Some ceremonies are intended to strengthen the marriage tie, some of them have direct reference to the separation of the bride from her parents, some again are symbolic in nature, emphasising other things, which one has to go through in married life. With the Hindu marriage being indissoluble and sacramental in nature, the observance of various marriage ceremonies is deemed necessary in as much as there is no difference between the written law and the actual practice of Hindus on this point.

No one is better qualified than the Vedic marriage ceremonies to preach duty, personal, social and health education emphasising morality and the virtues of marriage. The ceremonies give the couple the capacity to think about the consequences of their actions so that they can decide what is right and wrong. It provides a sense of self-esteem and a desire for self-improvement. The couple will find much greater stability for themselves and their children through marriage than they will through drifting in and out of marriage relationships with the children as the victims.

Ornaments and jewellery for married women

Golden armour, golden chariots, and decorations of gold and jewels are frequently mentioned in the Rig Vedic hymns. From Vedic times Hindu women have worn many ornaments on their ankles, which at every motion of the feet, produces a tinkling noise. Hindu and Muslim men and women wear armlets and bracelets of gold and silver alike. In carrying on their artistic skills the jewellers produce the most beautiful designs. The rose chains of Trichinopoly, and the snake chains of the Northern Karnataka all display great craftsmanship as does the silver filigree for which Cuttack (Orissa) is famous. The articles usually made in filigree work are bracelets, earrings, brooches, and chains, groups of flowers etc.

Enamelling, as applied in Indian jewellery, consists of an extremely fine pencilling of flowers and fancy designs in a variety of colours, and is invariably applied to the inner sides of bracelets, armlets, anklets, necklaces, ear-rings and sirpooch. The value of such a work depends on the fineness of the work, and often exceeds that containing precious stones. The finest specimens of this type of work can be traced in Delhi, Banaras and Jaipur.

Jewellery and women are inseparable from each other. At present tribal jewellery is very popular with modern girls. Gauri-Sangama necklace from Tamil Nadu is symbolic of the meeting of Gauri/Parvati and Lord Shiva. Hair braid ornaments, mangalmalai (the mango necklace) consisting of a gold set with pearls and precious stones, are famous from the Junagarh State and South India. Panchikan jewellery from Ahmedabad and the kohlapuri necklace with black beads from Maharashtra is famous all over India. Gems (rubies, saphires and emeralds, garnets, pearls) studded in gold are popular with people who can afford them.

On the wedding day the Hindu brides usually wear the following jewellery: Mangalsutra with black beads, bindi, bangles, rings and earrings. There is a lot of variety of Mangalsutras available in India. In Panjab the bride may wear the Kundan pendant set in 22-carat gold and held together with black bead chain or chains. In North India, women wear many bangles (called a choora) which is a symbol of her newly married status. The choora is a set of ivory bangles given to her by the maternal uncle of the bride.

In South India, the bridal necklace is called a Tali (a row of pendants composed of images of Shiva and Parvati seated on the Nandi bull. In Uttar Pradesh and Bihar, married women always wear toe rings (Bichwa). Sindhi women usually wear gold earrings studded with nine diamonds (navratan). Kashmiri women usually wears an ornament, called a Dhejoru, in her ears with a cord suspended from it at one end. Many Hindu/Sikh and Muslim women also wear nose ring at the time of wedding, as symbol of their married status.

Rings are used in Southern and Eastern Asia as signet rings, with a seal engraved, or for ornament, worn on the fingers, toes, wrists, ankles, or in the nose and ears. A ring is used as a married token in Europe and amongst all nations and in every age, the ring has been chosen as the suitable emblem of time.

Medicinal rings were at one time seriously believed in. Physicians were accustomed to wear finger rings in which stones were set, and these stones were credited with the possession of many virtues. Sometimes the patient was simply touched with the ring to cure; sometimes he put it on his finger to gain a magical power to cure. Many a patient has worn such a ring as a healing agent or to stop a haemorrhage. A wine-coloured amethyst, set in a ring, was a specific against intoxication and its consequences; a hyacinth stone acted as a charm to produce sleep; an agate had wonderful power in curing diseases of the eye; a jasper showed its value in cases of dropsy and fever; while a coral was an antidote against nervousness and causeless fears. The ring, with the title or name on it of the owner, was applied to documents in the place of a signature.

Wedding rings are always made of gold and exchanging wedding rings has been a western concept signifying promise of faithfulness of two individuals. A ring in modern times is proof of holy contract, in which the groom and bride promise to love and respect each other until their last breath. A wedding ring is usually worn on the fourth finger of the left hand, which is symbolic of touching the heart. European people believe that there is a particular vein in the fourth finger of the left hand that leads directly to heart, and that is the reason for wearing the ring on that finger.

Nose ornaments are called: Laung (nose pin), Nath (nose ring); ear ornaments are called: Jhumka, karna phool, bali, hina, boonde, pandadi. Neck ornaments are called: Tali (Tamil Nadu), chokar, malá, haar, kantha, mangalsutra, hussli (in Northern, Western and Eastern India).

Ankur panam (barley seed sowing)

In some parts of India, five pots of clay are used for sowing barley or other seeds and the pots are kept well watered and protected until the end of the marriage. When the seeds begin sprouting, four of them are kept in the four corners of the wedding altar, and the fifth one is placed before the household deity. If the wedding is performed outside one's home, the five pots are usually kept in front of the sacrificial fire on the altar. The four deities, after whom they are named, symbolise the sources of creation, preservation, annihilation, recreation etc. Seed sowing is the symbol for the spiritual flowing of the past into the future through the present.

The meaning of all the hymns, addressed to the various deities, is re-generation in man and nature. Thus, the union of the bride and groom stand for the union of heaven and earth, water and fire, life and love, along with that of body and soul.

Ancestral blessings and other rites

Being a sacrament, the ceremonies commence with the invocation of God's mercy and ancestral blessing by means of prayer and service (Sharadh). About a day or two before the wedding day, a brief Sharadh ceremony is offered to the manes for blessings at the commencement of the marriage preparations. The father of the bride and of the bridegroom does this separately in their respective homes. It is an appropriate beginning to all sacred actions. It signifies a very high level of society in which marriages are based not upon force, but upon consent, goodwill and agreeableness of the parties.

On the wedding day, the prospective bride and bridegroom have to perform various ablutionary rites (for example, a hygienic bath for the bridegroom and bride with powdered turmeric and other fragrant things in their respective homes).

In North India there is also a bangle (Choora/Chura) wearing ceremony. The red and white bangles signify the newly married status. They are traditionally a set of ivory bangles with inlay work. At present the bangles are usually made of plastic or acrylic. The bride usually wears it for forty-one days or depending on family tradition. In Rajasthan and some other parts of India women deck their arms with red and white or red and vivid green bangles. In Gujarat, gold and iron bangles are worn at marriage and in Bengal, bangles made of iron and conch shell are worn.

Puja (worship) is offered to the family deities, Lord Ganesha and a pot/pots filled with water representing the holy rivers, so that the wedding day will be auspicious and bring good luck to the bride and groom and to those witnessing the ceremony. After that the ceremony of *Sihra bandi* (a chaplet of flowers, or a piece of gold or silver fringe worn on the head by the bridegroom) for the bridegroom is performed in the company of family members, friends and relations. The bridegroom's party consisting of relatives and friends proceed to the bride's house/wedding hall. In the olden days the bridegroom usually rode a horse (now a days he comes by a car) preceded by a band of musicians and dancers to the wedding hall

Milni (meeting and receiving the bridegroom and party).

The bridegroom and party go to the bride's house or wedding hall. The gate of the bride's house/wedding hall is decorated with flowers and coloured lights, where the bride's family receives the bridegroom, his family, relations and friends. All of the wedding ceremonies with the arrival of bridegroom and party are held at the bride's house/wedding hall.

a) The bridegroom's father is the first one to be greeted and garlanded by the bride's father at the entrance or some other meeting point in the house or in the hall. Some relations are also introduced there by exchanging garlands.

b) In the next ceremony, the bridegroom is the chief guest and the bride the chief host. The bridegroom is welcomed by the bride's mother with a sacred light (light lit before an image in a temple) or the showering of flowers to bring good luck to the groom and ward off evil spirits if any are present there.

c) The bride's mother applies *Tilak* (a sandalwood or turmeric mark) on the bridegroom's forehead; it is a symbol of prosperity, lifelong happiness and success of the married couple. In some parts of India the Arti ceremony is performed.

Arati

Arati word is originated from Sanskrit *aratrika*, meaning the light. Usually on a plate of copper, a lamp made of rice-flour, earth or some metal is placed. It is filled with ghee (melted butter), or oil and lighted. Usually women and sometimes men take hold of the plate with a burning lamp, raising it as high as the person or idol, for which the ceremony is performed. The plate is rotated several times in front of the idol or person. The intention of this ceremony with humans is to keep away from them the evil influence of malevolence or jealous looks. When an influential person (King, Princes etc.) appears in public, the first thing that is done on their return home, is to perform the ceremony of Arati, as an antidote to the ill-designed looks which may have been cast upon them. The Arati was also performed in olden days when heroes used to return home victorious.

The Arati at the Puja ceremony (worship) is performed daily in the morning and evening at Hindu and Jain temples. It is a part of worship ceremony in front of the deity for blessings of good health, prosperity and peace in the world. The Arati ceremony in variant forms is also observed in other countries of the world.

Arati is also performed in some Sikh temples in front of the Adi Granth, as a concluding ceremony for an Akhand-Path (unbroken reading of the holy book from beginning to end) and also at the close of the evening service at a Gurdwara.

Jaimala

The bride will arrive at the *Milni* place in the company of her relations and friends. The bride and groom exchange garlands before entering the Mandap (temporary temple or altar erected for the wedding ceremony). Exchanging garlands signifies their acceptance of each other as lifelong companions. The meanings of the hymns recited by the priest at this ceremony are:

Bride says "My dear I accept you my future husband with this garland".

Bridegroom says, "May this garland bring you good fortune and enable you to become my wife".

Then the wedding party comes to the reception place with the bride and groom and their parents sit near the Mandap. The bridegroom is offered the seat of honour, facing east. At this point, the bride sits in another room until she is asked to join the groom in the Mandap.

The following ceremonies are observed at a wedding lasting between a few hours to the whole night.

Mandap and Wedding Day

Ceremonies start when bride and groom are seated in the Mandap (temporary temple or altar erected for the marriage ceremony) in the company of their parents and the priest.

1. Worship of deities. The parents of the bride request the approval of their guests for their daughter's wedding ceremony. The priest recites over twenty-four names of Vishnu and offer namaskar (salutation) to Vishnu. Gayatri Mantra (most sacred hymn) and the Gayatrishiras Mantra are also chanted by the priest and salutations are offered to Ganesha, Vishnu and Lakshmi, Shiv and Parvati, to Indra and Indrani, to the deities of the family, village and place deities, deities presiding over this ceremony and all other learned persons. A large number of names of Lord Ganesha are uttered for success in all undertakings. The parents of the bride and groom offer worship to the God Ganesha, the Mother Goddess, the nine heavenly bodies and to of the water vessels and pray for the bride and groom so that they can fulfil the aims dharma, artha and kama in married life.

The ceremony itself is a collection of rituals, performed by the bride, bridegroom and their respective parents and some relations. The priest chants mantras (hymns) from the Vedas and uses the following things in Puja (worship) ceremonies:

Fresh flowers to signify beauty; coconut to signify fertility; rice, sugar, and other grains to signify food necessary for the sustenance of human life; ghee (clarified butter) to feed the sacred fire; kumkum (red powder) for good luck and for marking the forehead on auspicious occasions.

The parents of the bride offer worship to Lord Ganesha, *Brahmin/Brahman* (the creator God of the Hindus), and other deities. Lord Ganesha is invoked first, by the priest, and is offered puja (worship). A little water is taken from a water container in the right hand and sipped to signify the purification of the soul. Water is sprinkled to purify the Mandap, and is also used frequently during the ceremony to bless the couple. Incense, lights and camphor are burnt and waved before the deity followed by *pradakshana* (circumambulation), especially in a temple flowers are also offered.

Each of these acts has a meaning. Sprinkling of water and sipping suggests purification of oneself and their surroundings. Water is sipped, for self-purification, from the right hand as the priest speaks the three names of the Lord Vishnu (Keshava, Narayan and Madhava). On the fourth name, Govinda, water is allowed to trickle from the right hand into the copper dish.

Picking flowers with all five fingers does the offering of flowers, as they are symbolic of what our five senses do. They are brought towards the heart and then placed at the foot of the icon. This symbolises the offering of one's atma (soul), mind and heart to God. Food from the house is offered as a thanksgiving for God's bounty. The breaking of the coconut symbolises the destruction of one's ego. The offering of coconut and betel leaves (symbolises fertility) asks God for the blessing of children. Here there is no mention of boy or girl. During the Vedic period male and female children were welcomed and given equal treatment.

2. Madhuparka (honey and yoghurt). The priest purifies the Mandap with some water and the father of the bride dips a flower or grass in the water within the Kalsha (water container) and with it touches the bridedgroom's head, throat, eyes, ears, shoulders, arms and heart. The priest blesses him with long life and good health. Madhuparka is also known as the Dvar puja (door-worship), which is synonymous to reception. Here the bride, her parents, relations and friends, receives the bridegroom. In this ceremony the bride says:

"Here is the seat, kindly accept it". The bridegroom accepts it with thanks. Then the bride says, "Here is water, kindly wash your feet".

The bridegroom accepts it with thanks.

Then the bride says, "Here is water to wash your face and to drink, kindly accept it."

The bridegroom accepts it with thanks.

Then the bride gives Madhuparka (mixture of honey and yoghurt) and the bridegroom receives it with thanks. In some parts of India the father of the bride gives some honey and yoghurt with the words: "I give this honey and yoghurt to the bridegroom who has completed his studies and has come to my house to seek my daughter in marriage. While the bridegroom is eating honey and yoghurt the priest recites the following hymns:

Om Gananam tva Ganapatim havamahe
Kavim Kavilnam upamas ravastamam
Jyestha rajam brahaman brahamanaspata
A nah shrnvann utibhih, sida sadanam

(Rig-Veda: 2.23.1)

We call upon you, the leader of the assembly of Gods (Ganesha), the great scholar, and the knower of the Brahman. Please hear our prayer and grace this place with your all-protecting presence.

Madhuvasta ritayate madhu kisharantu sindhavah
Madhvir nahy santv osadhih.
Madhu naktam uto sasi madhumat parthivam rajah
Madhu dyaur astu nah pita.
Madhuman no vanaspatih madhuman astu Suryah.
Madhvir gavo byhavantu nah.

(Yajur Veda Samhita 123.27)

May the breezes be sweet and pleasant, may the river flow with sweet waters, may the herbs give us sweet fluids, and may the night and dawn be sweet and comfortable to us.

May the earth be sweet, may our father sky be sweet, and may the plants and fruit provide sweet juices. May the sun make us healthy and our cattle give us sweet milk.

Gauri Puja. In some families, after Ganesh Puja, the bride goes into a private room to offer worship to Gauri (Parvati) and Shiva, praying to be blessed with healthy children, a long married life, prosperity, and good health.

The bride offers great hospitality to the bridegroom as if he is already a part of the family. At this time, the priest recites the following phrases:

Om Bhur Bhuvaha Svah - Sweets are the breaths of winds and flow of rivers. Let our hearts be full of sweetness for us. Night is sweet and so is the dawn. Sweet is earthly sand. Let our sky, vegetable kingdom be sweet for us and sweet be the sun who is the source of life, warmth and vegetation.

In short, the bridegroom is given a seat of honour and offered a little honey and yoghurt by the bride or her father who welcomes him to his house/wedding hall. The priest chants some benedictory phrases - divine blessings on everyone for earthly prosperity.

3. ***Kanyadan* (the gift or giving away of the bride by her parents) and *Patnigrahan* (acceptance of the bride)**. It implies handing the bride over by her father to the bridegroom. This custom is common amongst Hindus, Christians and Muslims, and means that the bride herself cannot provide herself to the groom, even of her own free will, in a sacramental form of marriage.

The ceremony of Kanyadan is one of the most important rites of marriage. The bride's parents perform a worship of the groom. Prayers for the vitality of the senses and organs (eyes, ears, heart, throat, head, and arms) are offered. The groom is offered honey and yoghurt, signifying sweetness and coolness in dealing with the bride.

The bride stands facing the bridegroom in the Mandap holding betel leaves, betel nut, rice grains and a flower in her cupped hands, and the priest touches their foreheads with the Kalasha (water pot). The bride's father touches her hands and asks the groom if he accepts the responsibility of being her husband. The bride's father says, "I give you my daughter in marriage - promise to be moderate in observance of Dharma, Artha and Kama". The groom touches the bride's right shoulder with his right hand and accepts betel nuts etc. from her. He promises to protect and maintain the bride, to appreciate her merits and forgive her shortcomings. The father of the bride at the time of giving her away also says, "Please accept this well educated, bedecked daughter, named so and so, born in such and such family". The groom accepts and grasps the hand of the bride. The bride is given away by mentioning the names of the fathers and forefathers of both sides. Now they are ready to become husband and wife and offer joint oblation to the fire. They jointly recite the following verse:

"Let all present here knows that our hearts have mingled together like water. Let breath, let God, the Gods, the Goddess of learning keep us joined". The relations and guests then say 'God has made you husband and wife and may God give you both a long, happy, healthy and fruitful life.'

The wedding knot (the end of bride's veil/scarf is tied to the end of the scarf on the groom's shoulder) is tied to signify the union of the bride and groom.

Sometimes the hands of the bride and bridegroom are tied together and the ends of their garments are also firmly knotted, indicating their unification forever. Prayers are said so that the union will be as firm as Lord Indra and Indrani, Vibhavasu and Svaha, Soma and Rohini, Nala and Damayanti, Vaisravana and Bhadra, Vasistha and Arundati, Gauri and Shankara and lastly as between Vishnu and Lakshmi. Each of these renowned unions in Hindu mythology has an auspicious notable feature, all of which are invoked here.

After this ceremony the bride and groom sits around the sacred fire and promises between the groom and bride are made. As a token of maintenance throughout life, the husband promises to fulfil the economic needs of the wife, enjoy with her their wealth and prosperity, and live happily for one hundred years.

4. Mangala Ashtaka (verses of blessings). In some parts of India, blessings are given to the couple at this stage as well. The bridegroom stands facing west. A cotton or silk cloth with the symbols of Om and the Swastika is held by two close relations/friends of the bride or groom as a screen in front of the groom. The bride is guided by the maternal uncle and made to stand opposite the bridegroom. Due to the screen they do not see each other. Rice grains coloured with red Kum Kum are distributed amongst the guests. The priest chants eight verses of blessings, from the Puranas. The verses are in praise of Lord Ganesha, the Brahman (Supreme spirit), etc. to bring good luck, health and prosperity to the couple After this the screen is removed and the bride and groom garland each other and put a few grains of rice on each other's head.

5. Akshataropana (wish fulfilling). The bride and groom support each other with their wishes - the bride wishes to have good luck, happiness and prosperity in life. The groom says, "*I will help you in achieving them*", and puts some rice grain on her head. The bridegroom also wishes to fulfil his Dharma obligations, and be happy and prosperous in married life. The bride puts some rice on his head and says "*I will help you in achieving them*".

6. Sutra veshtana (Bride and groom fasten a thread on each others wrist). The bridegroom ties a cotton thread coloured with yellow powder (turmeric) on the left wrist of the bride, and the bride ties a similar thread on the right wrist of the bridegroom. This symbolises their marriage bond, and the hope that their marriage will become dutiful, fruitful, prosperous and affectionate. The priest chants Mantras (hymns) throughout the ceremonies. This ceremony does not take place in some parts of India.

7. Panigrahana. The bridegroom takes in his right hand the bride's right hand and promises to be a good husband and prays that they live happily for ever in life.

The sacred fire (Agni) is lit and the couple takes their marriage vows with Agni as their witness. It is believed that fire is the first manifestation of Brahman (the One God creator of the universe)

8. Vivah Homa (marriage and vows before the sacred-fire). Agni sathapan (lighting the sacred fire). All the auspicious ceremonies are performed in the presence of sacred fire (Agni). The priest usually purifies the Havan (an oblation) materials by sprinkling holy water with two blades of grass. Some sacred wood (Banyan, Pippal, Mango etc) and camphor is put into the metal container (Havan kund) to ignite the fire. The bridegroom is asked to say these words (Om bhur bhuvah svah) in order to establish the sacred fire, Yojaka by name, in the metal container. O sacred Agni, of shandilya gotra, having a banner with the Ram emblem, being in the east in front of me, grant me a boon. The bridegroom now makes an offering of the two darbha (grass) blades to Skanda in the fire. Taking the five sticks of sacred wood, an oblation is given to Jataveda Agni. O Jatavada Agni, this wood fuel is your atman (soul). May you burn vigorously in order to increase your power. Similarly, may our children, cattle, and our knowledge of the Brahmin increases. With your grace, may we be blessed with plenty of food and water.

Some clarified butter and wood is placed repeatedly on the Agni to produce flames during the ceremony. The priest keeps on reciting Mantras (hymns) and samaghri (a mixture of herbs, clarified butter, rice grains) is offered to the sacred fire.

The bride sits on the right side of the bridegroom before the sacred-fire facing the East. The priest chants Mantras and asks the bride and groom to repeat the Mantras (hymns) after him. Various prayers and requests are made to the sacred-fire for their good luck and prosperity.

9. The bridegroom offers the seven oblations of ghee (clarified butter), while the bride touches his right hand with her right hand to participate in the ritual. The first oblation is given to Prajapati (Lord of creatures, a progenitor, and creator); the second to Agni, the third one to Soma (a sacred plant), and four more ghee oblations are offered to Agni to complete the main Havan. Oblations are offered to Agni to purify their lives, and protect their children and grandchildren.

10. Roasted millet and ghee (clarified butter) oblations are offered by the groom and bride to the sacred fire for success in their marriage and strengthening the bride's relations with the bridegroom's family.

11.Stone treading ceremony. There is a stone-slab on which the bride is asked to put her right foot and she is told to be firm like a rock to protect her and the groom's family's honour.

12. Agniparinayana or *Phere* (going around the fire). The bride and groom circumambulate the sacred-fire and water vessels (representing holy rivers), and promise to love each other, have children and live happily for a hundred years. According to Vedic rites, the couple sit before the sacred fire facing east in the Mandap, and the bride sit there on the right side of the bridegroom.

The bride's brother puts samaghri (herbs, ghee and roasted rice) into the hands of the bride and groom. They give three oblations to the sacred fire as the priest recites the Mantras. The bride has offered oblation to Agni, Varuna (Vedic deity) and the Sun God to strengthen her ties with her husband's family.

The bride and groom walk around the sacred fire seven times to take their seven wedding vows. First the bride will lead the bridegroom and walk clockwise three times around the fire. The bride will say the following hymns (mantras):

You are Sky, I am Earth. You are the melody of the Samaveda, I am the verse of the Rigveda. Let us marry, have children and live for a hundred autumns.

Secondly, the bridegroom will lead the bride and walk four times around the sacred fire clockwise and says the following hymns:

I am Sky, you are Earth. I am the melody of the Samaveda, you are the verse of the Rig-veda. Let us marry, have children and live for a hundred autumns.

The priest keeps on reciting Mantras and samaghri (mixture of herbs, clarified butter, rice grains) is offering it to the sacred fire. The circumambulation may be explained as being indicative of the respect shown to Agni (fire God), seeking its grace in respect of good progeny, bestowing riches, protection from evil spirits etc.
The bride offers worship to Agni, Varuna (Vedic deity) and the Sun God for strengthening her ties with groom's family.

13. Saptapadi (seven steps ceremony). The seven-step ceremony is essential for the completion of the marriage ceremony. Without it, a marriage can be declared null and void. It is performed to the north of the sacred-fire in a straight line. The priest makes seven small heaps of rice, about a foot apart, in a line to the north of the sacred fire. The couple stands side by side. The bride stands on the right side of the groom. The bridegroom puts his right hand on the bride's right shoulder and walks together. When the bridegroom speaks the Mantra (hymn) the bride and groom take a step forward with their right foot and bring their left foot forward to stand still. Each step is taken with the right foot in a slow walk - as the Mantra is recited. They take the seven steps together, and each step implies the following vows. Before each step the bridegroom says:

i) Take the first step for the sake of food and livelihood.

May God be your guide? Support me in my endeavours and follow me in my vows, etc.

ii) Take the second step for power and strength. Support me in my endeavours and follow me in my vows, etc.

iii) Take the third step for wealth and prosperity. Support me in my endeavours and follow me in my vows, etc.

iv) Take the fourth step to increase our happiness. Support me in my endeavours and follow me in my vows, etc. etc.

v) Take the fifth step for children and may they live to a ripe old age. Support me in my endeavours and follow me in my vows, etc.

vi) Take the sixth step for seasonal pleasures. Support me in my endeavours and follow me in my vows, etc.

vii) Take the seventh step for close union, life-long friendship, happiness, and companionship. Support me in my endeavours and follow me in my vows, etc.

Thereafter the bridegroom says to his bride: "Be my companion in achieving the seven objects of married life. I promise to be your friend and our friendship will be the source of our happiness". Now the bride sits on the side closest to the bridegroom's heart (left side).

14. Homa – Yajna, completion of ceremony. One more oblation (Auhoti) is made to Agni. The remaining ghee (clarified butter) in the container is then offered to Gods as one oblation. The bridegroom is asked to touch the water in the vessel kept north of the fire and offers a prayer to the holy water for blessing. The priest sprinkles the holy water with a flower or grass blades in all four directions and also on the bride and groom and guests sitting in the Mandap. In some families it is customary for the couple to apply the holy ash from Agni to their foreheads. The couple then stands and pray to Agni and the priest sprinkles the couple with holy water with a flower, and blesses with riches, success and happiness. Here the bride's parents bring the ceremony to a close.

15. Agni prarthana (prayers to Agni). Now the couple will stand and offer prayers to the holy Agni. (O) Holy Agni, you are Om incarnate. I bow to you to allow us to complete the Yajna (sacrifice). Grant me faith, intellect, success, understanding, learning, wisdom, riches, long life and health. The priest completes the marriage ceremony by blessing the bride and groom with long life, riches, success, peace and prosperity. The bride's and groom's parents also pray to god for long life, riches, success, peace and prosperity of the newly weds.

Local customs in some parts of India. At this stage many local customs are performed in conformance with the marriage ceremonies.

i) After the Saptapadis, in some parts of India, the bride is sprinkled on her head with holy water. By this ceremony, the bride is supposed to be free from physical troubles and sanctified for the married life.

ii) The husband touches the heart of the bride reaching over her right shoulder. The heart is the centre of feelings. By touching it the husband symbolically tries to rouse them and make them flow out to meet his own heart and thus unite them in the world of happy marriage.

iii) In some regions the bride is asked to sit on a red bull's hide, as it is symbolic of fertility and prosperity.

iv) The hair-loosening ceremony is also one of the minor items worth noting. The bridegroom takes the bride to a private room and there unties the knot of her hair of her head with these verses: "I free you from the life of celibacy, and we shall live a life of righteousness and charity. I am marrying you and your maidenhood comes to an end by my touch of your hair".

v) The tying of an auspicious yarn, wearing of garlands, tying the garments of the bride and bridegroom, touching the cup of a Banyan tree, touching the nose at the arrival of bridegroom, and applying some curd on the chest of the bridegroom etc. These ceremonies are not mentioned in the Grihyasutras.

vi) Mirror. The bridegroom places a mirror in the bride's right hand with an appropriate mantra, and it enables her to comb and dress her hair and see her own decorated and beautiful face. Holding the mirror is symbolic. One's own reflection in the mirror must have served as the basis of the concept of the double, the soul.

vii) Gold. Reference to gold occurs in the context of a ritual-bath, which the bride takes at the time of marriage. On her head is placed a small circle of twisted darbhas (*grass*). Over it is held the yoke-hold, with a piece of gold kept in it in such a way that the water for the bath (actually meant for lustration) flows through it touching the gold. This procedure is accompanied by various Mantras (hymns). Gold symbolises immortal life. Gold is said to be Truth and the very Aditya (celestial deity). It symbolises vital energy and vigour. The yellow shining lustre of gold was believed to stand for the golden light of the sun, or the soft flames of the fire. After the bath, it is believed that she will possesses all the qualities of gold. At present gold represents for richness, happiness and prosperity.

16. Mangala - ashtaka (verses of blessing). The priest usually chants eight verses of blessing, from the Puranas, about good luck, happiness, peace and prosperity of the couple. The verses are also in praise of Lord Ganesha and Brahman (the one Supreme God of the Hindus), and request their blessings on the bride and groom. The priest chants various Mantras to complete the ceremony.

17. Mangala Sutra (necklace of black beads). The bridegroom ties a necklace of black beads on the bride's neck. This is a symbol of good fortune, love, affection and friendship for their whole life. The bride may give a gold chain or ring to the groom. The Mangalsutra is a sign of good luck and prosperity, and in some parts of India it should never be removed.

18. Sinduradanam. The wife seats herself on the left side of her husband who fills the parting in the middle of her hair with a bit of Sindur (vermilion). The Mantras (hymns) recited at this time refer to the wife as the symbol of all kinds of material prosperity and good luck to the groom's family.

19. Ashirwad (Blessings) or Pushpavarsha (shower of flowers). In some parts of India groom and bride touches the heart of each other with the following verse:

"I put thy heart into my vow. Let my mind be in accordance with thy mind. Please pay attention to my words. Let God join thee with me."

The husband then touches the bride's forehead and addresses the visitors and friends attending: "Here is my fortunate wife, please bless her before you go.

The father of the bride says "my daughter be a queen (Rani) to your husband's family (father, mother, sister and brother). May you prosper and live happy for a hundred autumns, winter and spring seasons". Guests then bless her with good luck, happiness and prosperity".

Finally flowers and rice-grains are showered on the newly weds by family, relations and friends. The couple then bows to their family elders and other elderly relations and guests for their blessings.

Thus the Hindu wife is not only a colleague or partner, but also an equal companion and a co-worker in all spheres of life. Any female in the house is considered to be Lakshmi, Goddess of fortune and good luck. In the Mahabharata it is stated:

A wife is half the man, his truest friend

A loving wife is a perpetual spring of virtue, pleasure, and wealth;

A faithful wife is his best aid in seeking heavenly bliss;

A sweetly speaking wife is a companion

In solitude, a father in advice,

A mother in all seasons of distress,

A rest in passing through life's wilderness

20. Doli. After dinner: Doli (departure of the bride and groom) is a touching ceremony, in which the bride leaves her parents house and starts living with her husband.

Manu allowed child marriage and also held the women in high regard. According to him, if people wanted to be particularly blessed, the father, mother, brothers, the husband, and his brothers should respect/worship the bride/ women and provide them with suitable clothing and ornaments. Where women are worshipped, there the Gods (all sorts of blessings) dwell in the house. In a house where they are not worshipped, there all the activities and religious performances prove fruitless. Where the women of the family are not kept happy, the family is soon ruined. The family where they are kept happy attains prosperity. Homes, cursed by women, who are not treated there with due respect are totally destroyed. Happiness reigns supreme in homes where the husband and wife live in harmony with each other. If the wife is contented and happy, the whole home is happy. There is no happiness in the home, if she is discontented, and unhappy. The wife is like Lakshmi, the Goddess of bliss in the house. If a wife does not behave like a Lakshmi, she is not justified in getting respect from other members of family.

In the end, the priest who conducts the marriage ceremonies receives a cow as his fees. In the past the cow was usually given, but at present some hard cash, clothes and eatables are given to the priest.

In the evening after the wedding, the couple enter their new home after bowing to the elders in the family. They place their right foot on the threshold. Her right foot pushes a pot filled with grain so that the grain will scatter into the house. This will bring food, prosperity and good luck to the family.

The following morning the bride is offered welcome with new clothes, ornaments and sweet dishes. She has a new status and a new home. In some families she is given a new first name and welcomed as a new member of the family.

21. Feeding ceremony. This ceremony takes place when the bride comes to the bridegroom's house. The husband consoles her and says that she is the queen of the house. She has the same rights here as his father, mother, and brother and sister. The following morning the bride is introduced to the regular home life. In the olden days, first the husband and then the bride partake of simple food as in the course of student life for three days and nights and sleep together on the ground, as indicated in the conception ceremony.

The couple takes their food together, according to local customs, and the husband says that I join you with me by the fetter of food, which keeps the body and soul together. As food is the source of life, similarly we become each other's source of life. On the fourth day they begin to live as husband and wife. The marriage creates a new bond between the husband and wife. They are united like two young plants, which are uprooted from two different places and are transplanted into a new one. They have to rear up this union by dedicating their entire energy in the direction of their common interest and ideal. The marriage is a sacrament, and the union is not of bodies but the union of souls, indissoluble even by the death of either party.

At this stage of the marriage ceremonies, a number of ceremonies are performed in accordance with the local customs and traditions. In some regions of India the bride is required to look at the sun if the marriage takes place in the daytime, and she is supposed to look at the Polar star if the marriage has taken place during nighttime. These ceremonies are suggestive of firmness in the married life.

Tribal, provincial, caste and local customs in various parts of India

Marriage by capture and purchase

Rakshas (demon) was the heroic marriage, where a woman, carried off as a prize of war, was married without consent of her father, usually by her captor. It was a custom permitted to Kashatriya Rajputs and therefore called Kashatriya form. It is still prevalent in some parts of South India, Eastern India (Orissa, West Bengal), Gujarat and Uttar Pradesh. In the marriage songs of these places, which are sung today when the bride departs to her new home, the groom is compared to a robber and is showered with abuse; in some places a mock chase and fight are enacted. Examples of this form are seen in the case of Arjuna and Subhadra, Krishna and Rukamani; the most famous historical instance was the abduction by Prithviraj of Samyugta, the princess of Kanauj. At the marriage of Kashatriya Rajputs all the ceremonies are the same as other Hindus, but some of them bring weapons used in warfare with much solemnity, accompanied by the songs of the women and by instruments of music. These weapons remain hung up in the most conspicuous part of the pandal until the festivities are ended. The guests offer them sacrifices, and worship them from time to time, and similar processions are made round them to those of the Sudras round the sacred fig-branch.

Among the Santal tribes of Orissa and West Bengal, marriages take place usually, mostly in January, once a year. The young people select their own partners. For a few days, all the couples for matrimony live in promiscuously; after which only are the separate couples regarded as having established their right to marry. The daughter is always considered as the property of parents and the wife as the purchase of the husband. The Khond tribe of Orissa is still very primitive. They believe in animal sacrifice at the wedding, offering the blood to their goddess, to ensure fertility of the soil. They still use bows and arrows to protect themselves against wild animals. Among the Khonds, when the price of the wife has been arranged and paid by the father of the groom - a feast is held in the village of the bride, and the girl is carried off by the bridegroom and a large party of his friends of both sexes with much singing and dancing. The ancient custom of capture of wives continues to have symbolic representation. The Gond tribe of Madhya Pradesh also pay for a wife, but practice forcible abduction of the bride, with a mock fight. Widows re-marry either to the younger brother of the deceased husband, or to some other man or relation. They do not marry within the village.

The custom of capture is also to be traced in the rite of lifting the bride over the doorsteps, which has prevailed in such different and distant races as the Romans, Red Indians of Canada, the Chinese, the Abyssinians, and the Philippine Islands. In India, when people became civilised, marriage by capture generally disappeared from the society. It continued, however, among some Rajputs, some tribal and remote areas.

Sudra marriage ceremonies in South India and some other parts of India are equally solemn as other ceremonies of Hindus mentioned above. A peculiarity of Sudra wedding is that a lamp is kept alight in a prominent part of the Pandal during the three days' festivities, the wick of which is composed of 108 threads. Among the Sudras also the number of cooking pots is restricted to ten. The Brahmin who presides at the marriage begins by breaking one or more cocoanuts in different directions and determines the future of the newly married pair.

Exogamy and Endogamy

The practice of marrying outside their own group is widely practiced in Hindus, but some take their wives from amongst their own people. Usually people marry with woman who does not invoke the same Rishi as their ancestor (gotra). Asvalayana Grihasutra says that no one should marry his or her daughter to a man belonging to the same gotra or family. All the tribes of Manipur and many other tribes in India do not marry in their own tribe, and the intermarriage of members of the same family is strictly prohibited. In some parts of Southern and Western India, the maternal uncle may claim the daughters of a family as wives for his sons. The cousin marriage and marriage to maternal uncle is prevalent in some families in Southern and Western India.

Polyandry

It prevails in Tibet, is common in the Himalayan and sub-Himalayan regions adjoining Tibet, valley of Kashmir, Spiti, Ladakh, Kishtwar, Garhwal, in the Todas of Nilgiri Hills, some parts of Coorg or Kodagu (Carnataka), in Sudras and some other castes of Malabar and Travancore. In Panjab, among Jat families too poor to bear the marriage expenses of all the males, the wife of the older son has sometimes to accept her brother-in-laws as joint husbands. Some people from the Reddi race of Tamil Nadu and the Nambudri Brahmins of Travancore allow only the elder son to marry in order to preserve their family property and lands. In Reddi families, men marry their sister's daughter, but an aunt does not marry her nephew. If a man refuses to marry his sister's daughter, his father's property descends not to him, but to the man who marries the rejected woman. The Nair woman has also only one married husband, but can receive any other man of her own caste.

Colours - Significance in Marriage

Red. Throughout north India red is a colour of energy or power. It is an auspicious colour - they say the very essence of energy. It is a colour of any festive occasions. Wedding invitations are written with red ink; the bride wears a red Sari, red sandals and many red bangles of ivory glass or lacquer.

White is associated with purity of the heart. In Karnataka, the whiteness of the cloth being in itself a sign of ritual purity. Some Indians also associate it with inauspiciousness. The auspicious and inauspicious associations of white are not mutually exclusive. Just as the pure mind is steady and devoted, so also the pure body is integrated with a caste and family line. In South India the white-garbed males are the basis of family continuity.

Yellow is an important colour for an auspicious occasion. It has connotations of good fortune and associations with a special type of beauty. In flowers, in turmeric, and in gold itself - one finds yellow associated with the good times or good life of a well-ordered Hindu life. In India the announcement of a good event is marked with turmeric. As the colour of gold, yellow also have association with wealth and prestige and prosperity. There is usually a game, which is played at weddings in which a bride and groom compete by fishing around in a vessel for a gold ring, or money. The vessels are filled with a mixture of five grains, areca nut, and some water. The object of the game is to grasp a piece of gold a symbol of the wealth and prestige competition.

Green is quite prominent in Mysore, but plays a minor role in the popular rituals. Green is the colour of living organism. In South India, some families prefer green Saris at the time of a wedding. It is also a colour of glass bangles customarily for a woman in her seventh month of pregnancy. Green also is inherent in the ritual use of germination of grains. The metaphor is established between new vegetable growth and human beginnings.

Black is an isolated colour, and has several unfortunate and unhappy connotations. If someone appears at an auspicious event wearing black clothing, people will think about grief. As an ominous colour, black is thought to have the power to protect one against that which it represents. It is believed to have the power to repel the evil eye. Thus it is used as a mark on the faces of children, and even occasionally beautiful women. The black glass bangles customarily given to a bride or a married woman in some parts of India are not to indicate an inauspicious condition, but rather to prevent misfortune from coming to her. In India it is customary for married women to wear their marital tali pendant or Mangalsutra on a string of black thread and black beads to prevent misfortunes coming to them. It is observed that while white threads are used to invoke the power of beneficent spirits, black ones are used to prevent the power of evil spirits. Thus one will find black playing a role in auspicious events, used to prevent the power of evil spirits. Thus one will find black playing a role in auspicious events, although it is not a dominant colour on happy occasions.

Turmeric in Marriage

Turmeric is a generally used as a purifying agent and also as an auspicious medium of transition in many rites of passage. It also has medicinal uses. Turmeric seems to be also a symbol of generation, perhaps the female's generative powers. Muhammadans, Hindus and Sikhs, after betrothment and before marriage, the body is anointed with turmeric paste. Amongst Hindus, some recent Muslim converts and Sikhs, when they for the first time wear a new cloth or dress, they stain its four corners with turmeric, to ward off the evil eye and guard against malignant spirits. Turmeric is always emblematic of good tidings; for a soldier to smear his clothes with turmeric denotes that he devotes his life as a sacrifice. Amba Haldi is the term applied to the dyer's turmeric. Turmeric drives its name from terra meritra. Turmeric is the ground tubers of Curcuma longa, C. rotunda, C. augustifolia, C. viridifolia, and C. zedoaria. It is extensively grown in India, China etc. for home consumption and for export.

Flowers and trees – importance

Fresh flowers signify beauty, and Hindus, Buddhist and Muslims use them in their worship ceremonies. The flowers of the Calotropis gigantea, jasmine sambac, Michelia champaca, Mesua, ferrea, form the ornaments with which Kama (God of love), ornaments his arrows. Clitorea ternatea is sacred to Goddess Durga; Jonesia asoca is sacred plant. Then flax plant is sacred to Lord Shiva. Hiniscus rosa-Sinesis is sacred to Goddess Kali; Jasminium pubescens is sacred to

Lord Vishnu. The flowers of Mimusops elengi are favourites for garlands. The Chrysanthemum Indicum has a favourite garland flower. Datura fastuosa and Nerium odorum is sacred to Lord Shiva.

Lotus is sacred to Lord Vishnu; Nelumbium speciosum, (Indian lotus) is sacred to Brahma, Vishnu, Shiva, and their consorts, Saraswati, Lakshmi and Parvati. The lotus flower among the Hindus enters into all the ornaments of brass vessels used in the temples. In Hindu theology, the lotus floating on the water is an emblem of the world; the whole plant signifies both the earth and its two principles of fruitfulness.

Rose tree/bush flower is much prized in India. The flowers of the rose have a great variety of colours. Its perfume is extracted for export. Rose is used for worship and to make its garlands.

Tilak, Bindi - importance

Tilak, Bindi or Tikka are words commonly used to designate the various marking, which Hindus apply to their forehead as an auspicious mark, or sign of sectarian affiliation. Such a mark (Tilak) is made on the forehead, arms, or chest, with red, yellow or white coloured minerals or with sandalwood paste. It is applied in many religious ceremonies or after ritual bathing or on a festive occasion. The Hindu devotee, who regards himself as the property of his God, marks himself with his sect mark. The general motive for applying Tilak is that it is considered auspicious and keeps an evil eye away from the person wearing it. In some parts of India, the mother of the bridegroom puts a mark of red-coloured paste on her son's forehead, and sometimes on that of the mare on which he is mounted, before he sets out in procession to the bride's home. If the occasion is of special importance for the person concerned, a Tilak can be made more auspicious by sticking a few grains of rice onto the red paste. At Rakshabandhan (Rakhi) festival a sister ties a coloured thread on around the wrist of her brother and marks his forehead with Tilak or Tikka, as a symbol of her brother's good fortune, success and happiness etc.

Sihra-bandi

It means a chaplet of flowers, or a piece of gold or silver fringe worn on the head by the bridegroom, all over India, at the time of marriage. The main reason behind this ceremony is to keep the groom away from the evil influence of malevolence or jealous looks.

Wedding Rings in India and in the Western World

The act of giving a wedding ring or the exchange of rings is at the heart of the church marriage service and is a part of its ritual and tradition in India. The wedding ring does not have to be a new one; it can be a family heirloom, an old or antique ring. You can follow fashion when choosing the wedding ring, but often a simple, traditional style proves to be the best choice.

It is not necessary for the bride to give the groom a gift, but a ring or some other item of jewellery often forms part of the ceremony these days.

The other things to keep in mind are the bride's dress, outfits for women attendants, dresses for the bridesmaids, outfits for the mothers of the bride and groom. The flowers are also a very important part of every church wedding. Usually there will be bouquets or posies for the bride and bridesmaids and buttonholes for the principal men, and the church and reception area will be decorated with displays. There may also be sprays and corsages for the two mothers, and the bride may wish to wear a head-dress of fresh flowers or attach just one flower to her hair or veil. Your wedding day will be one of the most memorable days of your life, so it is imperative that you have a beautiful set of photographs to remind you of it.

Wedding superstitions in the Western world

Bride

It is considered unlucky to marry on your birthday. However it is considered a very lucky marriage if the husband and wife share the same birthday, but they must be a year or two apart.

It is generally considered unlucky for the bride to make her own wedding dress — even professional dress makers do not make their own dress. It is even unlucky to try on the full bridal array too soon, especially if she sees herself in a full-length mirror. An old veil especially borrowed from an old happily married woman is luckier than a new one. The good fortune and fertility of the earlier marriages pass with the veil to its new wearer.

The colour of the bride's dress is supposed to be a faithful portent of the future.

1. White is a symbol of purity and virtues.
2. Green typifies youth, hope and happiness.
3. Red is the sign of vigour, courage and great passion.
4. Violet denotes dignity, pride and high ideals.

It is a good omen for the bride to leave her home by the front door with her right foot foremost. It is considered lucky if the bride sees sunshine, or meet a black cat or chimney sweeper on the way to wedding hall or church. However, in Germany every drop of rain is looked upon as a blessing on the marriage but cats are not considered lucky.

It is considered lucky if the bride is woken on the day by the song of a bird, and also if she discovers a spider in the folds of her dress. If the bride sees a lamb, a dove, a spider, a toad, or a black cat on her way to the church it is a sign of good luck.

It is bad luck for bride to break anything on her wedding day - especially a mirror. It is also a bad luck for the couple to meet in the morning before the wedding, but good luck if they smile at each other when they meet in the church. It is a bad luck for the bride to weep, before the marriage, but she may do so as much as she likes afterwards.

Bridegroom

All will be well as long as he does not see his bride in her wedding dress before he meets her in the church, and does not drop the ring before putting it on her finger. If she has to help him in this, he may expect to be ruled by her in the future.

In the Western world the following dates are reckoned to be especially lucky for weddings:

January	2	4	11	19	21	
February	1	3	10	19	21	
March	3	5	12	20	23	
April	2	4	12	20	22	
May	2	4	12	20	23	
June	1	3	11	19	21	
July	1	3	12	19	21	31
August	2	11	18	20	31	
September	1	9	16	18	28	
October	15	18	27	29		
November	5	11	13	22	25	
December	1	8	10	19	22	29

Wedding anniversaries common to all

Most couples like to celebrate wedding anniversaries with presents and a good meal in a restaurant etc. Traditionally certain materials are associated with individual years in the course of a marriage, the idea being that anniversary presents in those years should be made out of those particular materials. The list below gives the materials generally associated with each year.

Anniversary	Wedding
First	Cotton or paper
Second	Paper
Third	Leather

Fourth	Silk or flowers
Fifth	Wood
Sixth	Sugar
Seventh	Wool or copper
Eighth	Bronze
Ninth	Pottery
Tenth	Tin
Eleventh	Steel
Twelfth	Silk and fine linen or leather
Thirteenth	Lace
Fourteenth	Ivory
Fifteenth	Crystal
Twentieth	Chine
Twenty-fifth	Silver
Thirtieth	Pearl
Thirty-fifth	Coral
Fortieth	Ruby
Forty-fifth	Sapphire
Fiftieth	Gold
Fifty-fifth	Emerald
Sixtieth	Diamond
Seventieth	Platinum
Seventy-fifth	Diamond

Changing your surname common to all

A professional woman does not have to change her surname when she gets married, although it is generally expected and usually makes life a little easier when making joint social, legal or financial arrangements. If you do decide to change your name the following authorities should be the first one to be notified:

Employer, bank, building society, saving accounts, insurance companies, credit card companies, passport office (it is convenient if you change name on your passport), Inland Revenue, Department of Health and Social Security,

DVLC (Driver's Licence and Vehicle Registration Document), Doctor and Dentist.

Aims towards a successful and happy marriage

During marriage days one must try to be more than normal, tolerant, flexible, co-operative, and must work incredibly hard to make the wedding day pleasant, happy and memorable. Obstinateness and dictatorial attitude of anybody can bring death knell to the relationship of parties and happy memories of the day.

One should always forgive and forget. If you cannot forget then learn to forgive for a happy married life. Do not let your professional and educational qualifications enter into your married happiness. It is extremely unfair to your wife/ husband and putting a lot of strain on your happy married life, if you are working late everyday and attending meeting every evening, or staying away on weekend conferences or tours. Try to maintain a balanced life, as marriage is more demanding and complex than one can imagine, and it can easily bring out your bad temper and other bad aspects of your personality to ruin your marriage.

Remember you have to adjust to the new situation and make sure that you establish new healthy relationship with your husband or wife's parents and relations. Do not feel shy about saying the truth, as the truth will win in the end. Remember that the communication is the lifeline of successful marriage. Work towards mutual respect and do not make unreasonable demands and expect radical changes. Do not be ashamed to apologise for your mistakes or rude behaviour. Marriage is a learning process – develop qualities that make both of you more human, kind and gentle. Get some help if you cannot communicate to him/her the truth about his/her achievements or failures.

5.

The Funeral Ceremonies (Antyesti Samskaras) in Hinduism

The last sacrament in the life of a Hindu is the cremation with which he concludes the final chapter of his worldly affairs. It is well known that through the sacraments after birth one lives happily on this earth and through the rituals after death one hopes to reach the heaven. Therefore it is essential that the death ceremonies should be performed with great care. In olden days it was believed that the death was not the natural end of life, but an abnormal and shocking event. Soon it was realised that death was a natural thing and any one born has to die. The usual theory of the process of death was the separation of the soul from the body. Formal farewell was given to the dead, and even the actual barriers were put between the living and the dead. The dead were provided with food and other articles necessary for a traveller, so that he would resume his journey to the next world. The living relation wanted the dead to reach his/her destination peacefully and comfortably. The corpse was disposed of by means of fire, so that the dead, being purified, may be allowed to enter the holy place of the ancestors. As the next world was believed to be the replica of this world, everything necessary (food, clothes, jewellery etc.) for starting a new life was presented and the things were consumed in fire with the dead.

The main objects of the proper disposal of the corpse and the performance of all the rites and ceremonies connected with it are to free the survivors from the pollution of death and to give rest to the dead. Until these rites and ceremonies are duly performed, the soul of the man is not finally dismissed to its place in the next world. This belief was current in all the ancient people all over the world. The funeral ceremonies were very important amongst the ancient Greeks, Egyptians and the Hindus.

At the time of cremation, hymns were uttered with the object of sending the dead person to heaven. The ashes and bones of the dead were also scattered or buried or immersed in the Ganges or some river by uttering Vedic verses with the object of sending the dead person to heaven. In Hinduism the burial of the dead was not known except in the cases of very small children and ascetics.

Another very powerful motive for cremation was the desire to get rid of the ghost of the dead. It was believed that the house of the ghost was destroyed by fire and it was frightened away by its flames. Fire can burn forest, grass and anything else and was believed to be useful in burning away the dead also.

The most important factor in the custom of cremation was due to religious belief that Fire was regarded as the messenger of God on earth, and the carrier of oblations offered to the God. After a man died it was necessary to send his body to heaven through fire. Cremation is regarded essential for the welfare of the souls of the dead, except children (under the age of puberty), who are pure and sinless, and of the holy men, saints who are supposed to have overcome evil tendencies during their lifetime, and therefore a burial for them considered as harmless. In Hinduism cremation ceremony releases the soul from the body for its journey to heaven. It is believed that without cremation the departed soul hovers around in great distress as a ghost.

The Funerals

The closing moments of a Hindu's life are associated with a number of ceremonies. Usually when the symptoms of death become manifest in a Hindu, a spot is chosen on the ground where a new cloth is laid upon which then a dying man is laid. Then a priest or the nearest relative pours a few drops of holy water into the mouth of the dying man, by virtue of which his/her body becomes perfectly purified. Then certain mantras are recited, by virtue of which he is delivered from all his/her sins. Orthodox families still give a cow in charity so that it may lead the dying person into the other world of heaven. Some give ten different articles in charity for the well being of the dead. It is believed that a Hindu should not die on bed. It is a bad omen if he expires on bed, and in order to relieve the dying person of such a bad omen, it is essential to offer abundant alms and perform expensive ceremonies. As soon as the dying person has breathed his/her last, it is a recognised custom that everybody present must at once burst into tears. Then the corpse is washed, dressed properly and covered with a piece of white unbleached uncut cloth. Then it is removed on a cart or carried on a wooden cot, accompanied by mourning relatives and sometimes also with professional mourners, to the cremation ground. The chief mourner (usually eldest son) leads the mourners. The mourners express their grief and a farewell address usually presented to the dead.

The cremation begins by offering the corpse to the sacred fire for conducting the corpse to heaven as a sacrificial gift. Then, taking hold of lighted fire, the chief mourner or eldest son sets fire to the four corners of the pile. As soon as the flames have caught hold of it everybody retires. The mourners are told not to express grief and entertain each other by consoling speeches and virtuous tales. The mourners took their funeral bath to purge the pollution caused by the funeral fire. The pure fire was lighted up in the house to remove the impure fire. Then all the mourners were fed. To promote the dead person's future wealth some presents are given to the Brahmans and also to the poor. Some people also perform Homa (Yajna/Havan) after death to purify the house. Next day or after a few days ashes and bones of the dead are collected in an urn and immersed in some river or Ganges. The next ceremony is called shanty-karma or the pacificatory rites for the well being of the living. It is performed on the ninth or fifteenth day after death. On the eleventh day Brahmans and poor people were also offered food and money. On the twelfth day the ceremony of Sapindi-Karna is performed to unite the spirit of the dead with ancestors. In this ceremony special prayers to God and offerings to the dead person's spirit are made so that the spirit passes into the abode of the ancestors through the medium of Sapindi-karna ceremony. The last item of the funeral ceremonies comprises offerings of food, water and milk to the dead.

All the funeral ceremonies are based on the assumption that the next world of the dead is nothing but the replica of this world, and the needs of the dead are the same as those of the living. Therefore the dead person will need all those things, which he has enjoyed in this world. For this reason, in all the ceremonies prayers are offered for the enjoyment and welfare of the dead. The prayers for freedom from the cycles of birth and death are also offered. The rites are expression of human beliefs, sentiments, aspirations, hopes and fears, and they catered for human needs. Many natural forces, which were feared or respected, have become docile servants of man. The reverence with which the religious rites were performed is diminishing gradually. These rites are changing from time to time and assuming new shapes.

Shradha

The last act that follows formally constitute the responsibilities of dead man's heir. More particularly, Shradh rites are associated with funeral and post-mortem observances. They are usually homage to the departed ancestors. A lamp of kneaded flour — filled with ghee (clarified butter) or oil and with a cotton wick placed in it.

The lamp is lit and kept at a prominent place in the house (with photograph of the deceased) or where the dead man breathed his last. The lamp is kept lit usually for ten days, as it is presumed that the soul remain tied to this world during these days before it goes to the next world. It is believed that the lamp helps the soul to find its way to the next world. The first of its ceremony takes place on the eleventh day after death. Thereafter, every year similar services are held. For this many Brahmins are feasted and a lot of money is given in charity. Many prayers are offered to god for the well being of the departed ancestors. The object of the Shradh is to ask the body of the dead to release the soul away to heaven or the region of bliss.

6.

The Place of Guru (Spiritual Preceptor) in Hinduism

A true Guru is a man who is in the habit of practising all the virtues; who has the feelings of a father for all his disciples; who makes no difference in his conduct between his friends and his enemies, but shows equal kindness to both, whose chief duty is to enlighten the ignorance in which the rest of mankind is plunged. He must be perfectly acquainted with the four Vedas, Dharma-sastra, Puranas and all other religious texts. The word Guru means master or guide, or the persons of distinguished rank who are raised to a high position and invested with a character of sanctity, which confers both spiritual and temporal powers upon them. In ancient educational system of India the Guru received pupils in his own ashram (hermitage). The pupil gave him implicit obedience, worked for him in the household and paid him great reverence.

In sectarian belief a deity is regarded as the founder of a particular order, and he is thus the first guru (adiguru) of that order. The living guru is the embodiment of the founder-deity and he is thus the last in a line of succession starting from the god. As he is the deity incarnate, salvation is possible through him alone. After his death one of his disciples, earlier selected by him, becomes the guru. The need of a guru is dictated by the fact the divine wisdom can only be transmitted by one who had been divinely appointed to receive them. The guru is the only living flame of such truth and he can only enlighten a disciple with the divine knowledge. Celebrated gurus sometimes receive equal homage as given to the deity. For example, the reverence in which Cahitanya Maha Prabhu is held is equivalent to that paid to Lord Krishna. Usually living guru is also worshipped. Lights are waived before him, incense burned in his presence, hymns are sung and prostrations made. The guru is also worshipped by making offerings of flowers and money to him/her. Gift to the guru (guru-dakshana) is a great tribute from a devotee/disciple to the guru for the knowledge received. Usually it is believed that the knowledge received would not be fruitful if guru-dakshana (gift) is not given to the guru. Any gift (prasadam) in the form of fruit, flowers or food from the guru's sacred hands has the merit of cleaning both soul and body from all impurities. Usually gurus make tours of inspection in those places where their followers are numerous for collecting money through guru-dakshana (gift to guru), on the occasion of a birth, initiation, marriage and death ceremonies. Some gurus are married, but most are celibates. The gurus after discharging duties to their followers, and performed their daily ablutions and sacrifices, both morning and evening, the gurus employ the rest of their time in the study and contemplation of their sacred books. In the case of married gurus the office descends from father to son.

Temple or Mandir

The Hindu temple is meant to be a dwelling place for the god. The Hindu temple serves as a peaceful place where the devotees pray to the deity. Often groups of images of Ram - Sita, Lakshman, Hauman; Vishnu; Krishna-Radha and Shiva-Parvarti etc are found in temples. The better-known temples of the Hindus are of Dwarka or Somnath, Triputi, Minakshi temple of Madurai, Tanjore, Jaganbnath etc. Originally temples were built of timber in 3rd century BC with elaborate woodcarvings of animals and human beings as decorations.

Later the stone temples were built in the 8th century AD. By the 13th century AD most of the beautiful Hindu temples were built. Some famous temples and places of worship are:

Ajanta

The world famous cave paintings of Ajanta are in Maharashtra, about 250 miles northeast of Mumbai, and is the site of twenty-nine Buddhist caves excavated in the rock. The caves are older than those at Ellora, and situated in a forested ravine of the Shyadri hills. The surroundings of Ajanta are extremely beautiful, the ideal place for a monastic life. The caves consist of chaityas (places of worship), viharas (monasteries) and galleries about one-third of a mile in a sickle-shaped curve along the face of a cliff. Dating from 200 BC to 650 AD the caves are the work of early Chaulakya kings. The caves are meant to have housed about 200 monks (artists, craftsmen and labourers). The paintings on the walls of caves tell the life-story of the Buddha, his previous birth – showing the progress of the soul, royal court settings, family life, street scenes, animals and birds, and life and culture of the people of that time. There is unfolded panorama of dancing girls, boating and hunting scenes, bullfights, beggars, elephant and monkeys, flowers, and intimate details of women in their bedrooms. There is a river Tapti in the hills below, and originally the entrance to the caves was along the riverbed.

There are two groups of caves, five of Hinayana Buddhism and the rest of Mahayana Buddhism. The caves are embellished with horseshoe windows, colonnaded aisles, vaulted and ribbed roofs, antechambers, cisterns, and finally chiselled statues, reliefs and friezes. The paintings on the walls of the caves of Ajanta have earned worldwide renown. Ajanta murals tend to be decorative and represent the perfection of the primitive and linear approach to art. By the beginning of the eighth century the caves were abandoned by the monks and lost to the world. Some soldiers of the East India Company accidentally discovered them in 1819.

Ellora

A place of extreme beauty, near a trade route between Ujjain (Madhyapradesh) and the west coast, and can be visited in a few hours from Aurangabad (Maharashtra). At present it is in Maharashtra. It contains Hindu, Jain and Buddhist caves carved in the volcanic rocks at Ellora. They are one of the best in India. It is believed that many different priests who used these routes dug the caves. It is a sight associated with the exploits of gods and heroes, is today well known for its twelve Buddhist, seventeen Hindu, and five Jain viharas (monasteries), chaityas (places of worship) and cave temples, carved out of the rock. Some of the temples are two to three stories high. Their names: Das Avtars (Ten Incarnations 630 AD), (Ravan ka Khai (Ravan's excavations 640 AD), Sita ki nahini (Sita's bath 650AD), Indra Sabha (Indra's council 800 AD), Jagannath sabha (the council of Jagannath 850 AD). They all depict the well known stories of Hindu mythology. The remarkable features of these excavations include: the long and exciting colonnaded cloisters and lighting effects; the cyclopean guardian figures; the most beautiful architectural devices, such as a roof carved in imitation of ribs in the Buddhist Visvkarman cave; very rich mythological sculpture of lofty dimension and majestic conception; the people listening to the discourse of Buddha; the grace of flying figures; the sensual postures of couples and goddesses; and the great precision of detail in headdress and ornaments. These make this temple the centre of one of the most beautiful sights of the world. The most impressive structure in Ellora is the temple of Kailasnath (Siva's paradise) built by Rashrakuta (king of Malked). The copperplate in the temple declares with pride that such a beauty would not be found anywhere. The temple consists of an entrance gate, a

Nandi (Shiva's bull) temple, a circumambulatory passage around the main shrine, a linga shrine, and a chapel dedicated to five river goddesses, and five other shrines. There is an astonishing feat of craftsmanship that went into making this temple.

Khajuraho Temples

The name Khajuraho is derived from Khajur (date palm tree), which grows freely in the area. The temples are famous all over the world as thought provoking monuments of Indian sculpture and architecture. The temples were built under Chandela Rajput Kings between 950 and 1050 AD. The Kings were great patrons of art and architecture, and the heart of their architectural fame is the village of Khajuraho, about 5 km from Jhansi (Madhya Pradesh). They built about 85 Saivite, Vaishvanite and Jain temples and shrines, of which 25 surviving are among the finest in India. The temples were built of fine sandstone from Panna in colours ranging from pink to pale yellow. They were lost in forests for centuries, and accidentally discovered by a British army engineer in 1838. It is believed that Chandela kings were under the influence of Tantric Gurus when they built these temples. In Tantrism it is believed that the gratification of earthly desires is a step towards attaining the ultimate liberation (moksha). The interiors of the temples are richly carved with dwarfs, gargoyles and grotesques, as well as female figures of sensual grace. The exterior of temples has over 650 nude figures, mostly female, and also there are others depicting pictures of sexual union. Some believe that they illustrate the Kama Sutra, the sensuality outside the temple contrasting with the serenity within.

Jagannath Puri

It is in Orissa. The temple is the major attraction of the Puri and for Hindus, to remain here for three days and three nights is considered particularly rewarding. The three wooden figures of the deities (Jagannath, Balabhadra and Subhadra) stand in the centre of the temple. The temple is known as the white Pagoda (the Konark temple being the black Pagoda). Lord Jagannath's car festival commemorates Lord Krishna's journey from Gokul to Mathura. The other major attraction of Puri is the long stretch of golden beach. Local festivals are: Chandan Yatra (April), Rath Yatra (June-July), and Beach festival (November) one week of cultural shows, crafts and food stalls.

Minakshi temple of Madurai

The Nayak rulers built the temple in 1623-55. .Madurai's fame is based on its great temple.

Varanasi (Kashi or Banaras)

The sacred city of the Hindus. Variance derives it name from two streams (Varuna and Assi). It is one of the seven sacred cities of Hinduism. The Hindus usually like to go there once in their life time. Lord Shiva blessed this city with the boon that any person dying in the city would achieve salvation from the cycle of transmigration. The most important temples in city are Madhadasha, Dharahara, Vishveshvar, Vishvanath, the Golden temple of Shiva, Durga temple, Alamgir mosque and Gyanvapi mosque. Varanasi is the major centre of Sanskrit learning in North India. It is famous for ornamental brasswork, silks, embroideries and for the manufacture of glass beads. Places of interest are Raja Ghat, Assi Ghat, Panch Kosi and many other Ghats. All the Hindu and Muslim festivals are celebrated.

Mathura and Vrindaban

A land that takes its seat in both history and mythology, Mathura lay many claims to fame. It is the birthplace of Lord Krishna, the eighth incarnation of Lord Vishnu. Every bit of this area is wrapped in eternal devotion to Lord Krishna. There are many temples in Vrindaban devoted to Lord Krishna.

Hindu temple ceremonies

Buildings dedicated to religious worship are found in all parts of India. It is generally believed that no place should be inhabited where there is no temple, for otherwise the inhabitants would run grave risk of misfortune. The structure of the large temples, both ancient and modern, is the same. Their architectural designs are probably better examples of building compared to other ancient civilised nations. The temple in South India is often a self-contained unit like a little town. The temple, mandap, and subsidiary structures have a broad open courtyard, known as prakarma going around them on all four sides. Outside the prakarma and enclosing the whole area rises a high wall in the shape of a quadrilateral. In the middle of one or more of the sides of this enclosing wall rises a very high with richly sculptured gateway known as gopuram, which derives its name from the cow-gate of the Vedic village. It is usually noticed that in the North Indian temple the main tower is built over the shrine of the god, which is in the centre of the temple. In South India it is raised over the entrance gateways and is the most beautiful feature of the temple seen from outside. The typical gopuram (gateway) is oblong in plan and rises to a height of 150 feet. Outside the walled area is yet another open courtyard, with shrines, tanks for ablution, and subsidiary buildings, the whole of this area being enclosed within four walls having one or more gates. Sometimes there are about four such concentric walls, each with its gate, and each enclosing an open courtyard with many shrines.

The temple is mainly meant to be a dwelling place for the god. There is one essential element in the Hindu temple where the god and his consort in the form of an idol are installed. All other parts of he temple are additions and elaborations around this temple sanctuary. Parts of the temple are set apart for the preparation of sacrificial food, the recitation of mantras, the sacred fire, the storing of consecrated utensils and implements. Within the temple are subsidiary buildings (assembly hall, dancing hall, hall of offering, shrines dedicated to various deities etc). The highest form of devotion is the worship ceremony of Brahma in his purest form as the creator, ruler, provider, Lord of life and death. Ceremonial devotions may be performed by tending household fire, the recitation of texts, and the repetition of mantras, meditation or communal worship with hymns, prayers and sermons. In private worship some preparatory forms may be observed prior to actual meditation on the deity. Usually the worshipper sits in the crossed-legged posture and cleanses himself and his surroundings by purificatory mantras before worship/prayer or chanting of hymns. The order and the method of service are not uniform. Some of the services offered to the idol are also offered to one's guru, as he is regarded as representative of the deity. A fact worthy of remark is that the officiating priests wear their ordinary clothes in the exercise of their sacerdotal functions, which are newly washed for the purpose. The following are the chief ceremonies in a temple:

1. Awakening of the deity (Prabodha). Every morning the priest ceremonially opens the doors of the chamber, in which the deity is housed. The flowers used on the previous day are thrown and the chamber swept. The deity is gently roused from sleep. Apart from the nightly sleep there may be a midday sleep, while some of the major deities have long periods of sleep during certain months and therefore special arousal ceremonies are conducted on such occasions.

2. Bathing (snan). After awakening the deity may get his teeth washed, mouth rinsed, given a ceremonial bath and anointed with sandalwood paste, then dressed in fresh robes and decked in ornaments. Most of these sacred ceremonies take place behind a curtain between the worshipper and the idol, but at each of the procedure the priest tinkles a little bell, which he holds in his left hand to mark the stage of worship.

3. Invocation (the calling upon the deity by his name or appellative). Sacrificial offerings are placed before a fire; the bell is rung and a conch-shell blown to summon the deity.

4. Adoration of the deity on his presumed arrival. This includes welcoming of the deity; obeisance making or the reverent salutation. The deity is usually offered garlands, given a seat, washed his feet. Such services are also offered to a guru.

5. Circumambulation. The rite in which the worshipper walks around the image or the shrine where the god is housed. Usually in temples special ambulatories are provided to enable the worshipper or pilgrim to, perform this act of homage.

6. Gift-offering. This consists of various offerings of rice, grain and ghee (clarified butter) to feed birds. Other offerings include flowers, water, saffron, some spices, incense, camphor and aromatic vapours, betel, sandalwood paste to smear on the forehead.

7. Arti. Ceremony of waving the lighted lamp before the idol, in a clockwise direction, accompanied by chanting of mantras (hymns). It is to please the deity with bright lights and also to counteract the evil eye.

8. Prasad (sacrificial food). The food (rice, fruit, sweetmeats) is offered for seeking favour of the deity. Food offered to the guru is also called Prasad. All things touched by the deity or guru are given to the devotees, as they are extremely beneficial to them.

9. Request to the deity (Prarthana) for personal favours, and help in private matters.

10. The last part of the worship is to bid farewell to the deity for night's rest with appropriate hymns. The deity is enshrined on a portable altar and is carried to his bedchamber to join his wife.

In famous and larger temples the deity has many priests and attendants - who dress, feed and do many other things for the deity. The god is entertained by dancing, fanned by many fanners, bathed, garlanded and robed by priests. There are many elaborate ceremonies on some occasions like the changing of the golden thread. On big festival days the deity is taken in procession around the town in a special car like the Jagannath temple in Puri. The god's marriage is celebrated annually by carrying the idols (god and his consort) in the streets with the music and dance. This celebration is very popular in South Indian shrines. Usually people go to temple to pray and make a vow or pledge something to god in return to the fulfilment of some wish. People also offer something to the temple for the welfare of their family. Many temples and some trees are well known as wish granter through some rituals. If a wish were fulfilled then the wish maker would always try to fulfil it. The rich make vows to sponsor certain festivals, extension of the building or present some gift of gold or silver. In famous temples many pilgrims bring offerings of money, food, gold, silver, jewels, costly clothes and cows etc. to help maintain buildings and many people employed for doing various jobs in the temple. Evening prayer as prescribed by Hinduism has fourteen parts with proper rituals. During the rituals it is advised to chant Gayatri mantra 108 or 1000 times. If the time is short it can be shortened to the essential aspects.

Idol Worship

At some stage idolatry became an integral part of Hindu religion. The Vedic religion knows no idols. The Jabala Upanishads says, images are meant only as aids to meditation. It is possible that the Aryans had no images, but acquired them after getting in touch with the native Indian, and in due course became full-fledged idolaters themselves.

Later literature contains many references to image worship, and during the epic period the practice was almost universal. In the Ramayana we find Lord Rama making an image of his wife for household worship and also presenting an image of his household god as a coronation gift to a temple. The Mahabharata tells us that adoration of idols was common at that time.

Early Buddhism as preached by Buddha forbade the worship or the making of idols. After the death of Buddha his empty throne, his sacred footprints were used to help the worshipper to meditate on the presence of the blessed one. With the spread of Greek influence the Buddha image was introduced and the idols of Buddha were mass-produced in north Indian art, and soon spread throughout the Buddhist world.

From Buddhism, the Hinduism received great encouragement for idolatry, and people started making idols of Hindu deities for installing in temples and domestic shrines. Panini (350 BC) and Patanjali (200 BC) speak of image of a deity made for the purpose of worship and taken from home to home to collect alms from householders, who regarded these images in great veneration. The art of making idols was elaborated to make them look beautiful.

The material for making an idol have to be carefully selected, as each kind of stone, mineral or metal has a specific virtue and when used either alone or in combination brings specific potencies to bear on the place of its installation. Idols were made for festivals, made of clay, which can be dissolved when thrown into the river or sea after use. If wood is chosen it has to come from a special tree.

Images are made according to set norms or proportion an the divine attributes and powers are represented in its stance, number of limbs, the type of objects held in hands and the vehicle on which the deity is mounted.

Before the image can be used for worship in a temple, it has to be properly consecrated. On an auspicious day the idol is usually installed in a temple by the chanting of Mantras. The mere sight of it absolves one from all sin. It is believed in Hinduism that idolatry represents millions of broken fragments of god. Collect them together and you get the Indivisible Divinity (One Supreme God).

In fact image (murti), figure, statues or pictures of the gods are teaching aids for beginners, who need a physical object to concentrate their untrained minds on before they learn ro meditate properly, by concentrating their minds directly on god. Worshippers will clean the statues, pour milk over them, place flowers around them and burn incense near them in the hope of establishing a close bond with the god. In this way believers can establish a loving relationship with god.

To the orthodox Hindu the clay idol represent the very presence of the deity, but after worship when it is immersed in water it gives the feeling that it is an aid for worshipping the unknown god. Others, who hold that the One God is indivisible, believe that the making and worshipping of an idol does not take away from the divine unity. In fact idolatry represents millions of broken fragments of god. Collect them together and you get the Indivisible Divinity. Finally idol worship is not peculiar to Hinduism only. The Christians worship the Cross-, as they have the image of Cross in their minds. The Muslims keep the image of the Kaaba stone when they kneel and do prayers. The people of the whole world except a Yogis and Vedantins, are all worshippers of idols. They keep some image or the other in mind. Some people believe that by having faith in idol worship one can obtain, happiness, prosperity, peace, and attain god

Agni (Fire worship)

Agni is a god of fire (Latin, ignis or the old Slavic god Ogoni or Agoni), a deity of Vedic people originally worshipped by Aryan nomads of Central Asia. It is one of the most ancient and most sacred objects of Hindu worship and more hymns are addressed to him in the Rig Veda than to any other god. He is one of the three great deities – Agni, Vayu (or Indra), and Surya – who respectively presides over earth, air and sky, and are all-equal in dignity. He is considered as the mediator between men and gods, as protector of men and their homes, and as witness of their actions; hence his invocation at all solemn occasions, at the marriage ceremonies etc. He is the giver of happiness, prosperity and good things in life and a relentless opponent of darkness and evil.

In Vishnu Puran he is called Abhimani, and the eldest son of Brahma. His wife was Swaha; by her he had three sons (Pavaka, Pavamana, and Suchi), and these had forty-five sons; altogether forty-nine persons, identical with forty-nine fires. He is described in the Hari-vansa as clothed in black, having smoke for his standard and headpiece, and carrying a flaming javelin. He has four hands, and is born in a chariot drawn by red horses, and the seven winds are the wheels of his car.

In Agni Puran, Agni is the deity of fire. The Puran derives its name from its having been communicated originally by Agni (deity of fire), to the Muni Vashishtha, for the purpose of instructing him in the twofold knowledge of Brahma. It includes ritual and mystic worship, medicine and many other things etc.

Agni is the personification of three kinds of fire, namely, the sun, the lightning and the sacrificial fire. Hindus worship and treat it as a deity since it is essential firstly in the sun, secondly in the sacrificial fire which is lit to make the sun rise, thirdly in the fireplace in the houses where the food is prepared, fourthly on funeral pyres on which dead bodies are purified, fifthly in the Indian oil-lamps without which no one can see at night, sixthly in lightning and seventhly in distant stars.

Agni is born wherever a fire is lit, especially sacrificial fire. Agni is also the endless fire that destroyed the ancient forests of India to make room for the plough, because is a friend of mankind. Agni is also the fire of the sun and the fire of lightning. Agni has also good aspects, since he is a friend in every household. Indeed if there is no fire in the house, the lady of the house must be ill or have died. Agni is also the deity of marriage, as the bride and groom walk around the fire seven times on their wedding day to sanctify the marriage.

One day the sage Bhrigu carried away the wife of a man. Agni is honest and pure, has access to all homes and therefore told the aggrieved man where his wife was. The man went to Bhrigu's house and brought his wife back. Bhrigu in his anger cursed Agni: You, fire, will consume every piece of dirt on earth. Agni remonstrated that gods must always speak the truth and that Bhrigu was impure one. Bhrigu admitted his fault and added to his curse (which could not be removed) that the fire would make all things pure, even dirt. This is why the Hindus burn dead bodies to be purified by Agni.

Dyaus (Sky)

It is an early Indo-European deity of the sky or heaven. Dyaus means light, the sky or the sky god, often referred to as Dyaus-pitri or Dyaus-pita (sky as father). He may be identified with Greek antiquity. His wife is Prithvi (earth), the goddess of nature, the mother goddess who can be identified with the Greek Gaya, Together they are regarded as parents of the gods and human beings People worship it as they worship other sources of nature.

Earth (Bhu, Bhumi, Prithvi)

In the Vedas the earth is personified as the mother of all beings, and is invoked together with the sky. According to the Vedas there are three earths corresponding to the three heavens, and our earth is called Bhumi. In the Vishnu Puran she is represented as receiving her name from a mythical person named Prithu, who granted her life, and so was to her as father.

The Earth goddess before creation was at the bottom of the primeval ocean, and Brahma brought her to the surface in the shape of a many petalled-lotus flower, which opened as soon she reached the light. Brahma, the creator, is depicted seated on the rising lotus absorbed in meditation.

Many people in India worship the earth as a tree-goddess. Some Indians also worship Savitri as the earth-goddess since she conceives children from her husband after he has died. Prithvi (Vedic goddess), wife of Dyaus (sky), mother of Indra and Agni is comparable to the Geek goddess Gaia, and the Roman Tellus. Men have to work hard ploughing the earth before she will give them grain, fruit etc. Some as the mother of all gods regarded her, and she is also the mother of all people, plants, trees, animals etc. The name Prithvi is used in the meaning of nature, like the Roman goddess Natura – who gives birth continuously. Prithvi is considered gentle and kind for the fruits she gives to every one.

Moon (Soma, Chandra)

In the Puranic mythology Soma, as the moon, is commonly said to be the son of the sage Atri by his wife Ansuya, The simple minded Vedic people worshipped the powers and phenomena of nature and found in it something divine to worship it for their welfare and prosperity. Another name for moon is Chandra (the Moon-god). Somvaar (Monday), is named after Soma. His symbol is silver crescent. It is very auspicious to be born at full moon day. Soma rides through the sky in a chariot with three wheels, drawn by ten horses as white as Jasmine flowers. The moon is also called Shasha (hare), since it is believed that the man in the moon is a hare, in Indian folklore. Thus the hare is regarded by some as a moon-deity.

Vayu (Air, wind)

The god of wind in the Vedas is often associated with Indra, and rides in the same celestial car with him, Indra being the charioteer. The chariot has a framework of gold, which touches the sky, and is drawn by a thousand horses. According to Nirukta there are three gods connected with each other. Agni, whose place is on earth; Vayu or Indra whose place is in the air; and Suryá whose place is in heaven. Vayu is the reputed father of Bhim (one of the Pandu brothers) and of Hanuman.

Vayu is the god of the soft breeze and breath everyone takes, that who gives life to all people, animals and other beings. He is the god of life and also god of violent character, restlessly travelling all over the earth. He broke off the top of the Mount Meru and threw it into the ocean – thus creating Sri Lanka.

Varuna (god of water, seas and rivers)

One of the oldest of the Vedic deities, a personification of the all-investing sky, and the maker and upholder of heaven and earth. As such he is the king of the universe, king of gods and men, possessor of illimitable knowledge, the supreme deity, which deserve a special honour and worship. He is a god of water (ocean, rivers). In the Puranas, Varuna is sovereign of the waters, and one of his accompaniments is a noose, which the Vedic deity also carried for binding offenders: this is called Naga-pasa, Pulakang or Viswajit. Varuna dug the riverbeds and the oceans. Out of the ocean arose Brahma, ready to create the world. Varuna fixed the stars in the night-sky and makes them vanish at dawn. Varuna makes the moon walk in brightness.

Varuna possess the secrets of the creation, which he taught to his son, the sage Vassishtha born from Urvasi's soul. Varuna assigned to every planet his path and taught the winds to blow and birds to fly. He is the keeper of heaven and earth and his own capital is Pushpa-giri (flower mountain). His other names are Jalpati (Lord of the waters) and Yadahpati (Lord of the living beings in the water).

Salutation and greeting etiquettes

In Hinduism it is common that a junior greets the senior and an inferiors greets the superior by performing namaskar (salutation), which consists in joining both hands, touching the forehead, and then putting them above the head. It means respectful greeting, my lord - upon whom the superior or senior will extends his or her hand, partially open and says ASIRVAD (God bless you long and healthy life). Another very respectful manner of greeting is to extend both hands towards the feet of him/her whom you wish to honour, or to seize his knees while you bend yourself to touch his/her feet. This is a very common mode of greeting between a son and a father/mother, or between a younger and elder brother or daughter-in-law and father-in-law or mother-in-law or any other elder member of husband's family. Children salute their parents in the same manner and stand upright before them. Whenever relatives or good friends meet after a long time, they clasp each other in their arms and take hold of each other's chin feeling very happy. After sneezing a Hindu never fails to exclaim Ram, Ram or God bless you. The most reverential form of salutation is the sashtanga (eight limbs) when the eight parts of the body (two hands, two feet, two knees, foreheads and breast) touch the ground and expresses great respect like a student to a teacher or a subject before a sovereign. During Muslim rule in India the custom of close embrace began – a person puts his arms around the other and hugs him closely. People also casually raise hands and wish good luck to each other from some distance. It is perhaps very common form of salute today. Handshake is also very common in all parts of India, in which they shower blessings on each other and ask about each other's welfare. It is also a mark of respect when women turn their backs on men whom they hold in high esteem. At any rate, they usually turn away their faces or cover them with their saris or scarf (dapatta). Any one who sees a person of high rank coming towards him usually say Namaskar and bend down as a mark of respect. It must be admitted that the custom of etiquette and social politeness are much more observed by Hindus than they are by people of Europe.

Ji. This word is a corrupted form of the Sanskrit word *Jiv* meanig life, soul, self, spirit. Good manners dictate that it should be used as a form of honorific address = O worthy one or a beloved friend, Sir, yes, to welcome etc. Now a days it is used by one Indian to another Indian and also by family members to each other and between friends as a sign of respect. It is usually used as a suffix to a name, e.g. Joshi Ji, Arki Ji, etc.

Worship of animals

In olden days it was believed that anything that can be useful to a man was worthy of being worshipped. Thus the Egyptians worshipped the bull Apis, the ibis, the crocodile, beetles, snakes etc. As for the Hindus they worshipped monkey, the bull, cow, the bird called garuda, and snakes etc.

Various classifications of the animals are given in the Upanishads, Puranas and many other works (Patanjali, Charaka, Sushruta). According to legend Lord Siva created the different species by assuming their characteristic. Brahma, the creator, was also responsible for the creation of animals, as he concealed in each species a great secret. Many Hindu gods are associated with an animal vehicle. When Lord Vishnu appeared on earth to save the world from some invincible demon he came in an animal shape (fish, tortoise, boar or lion, since it was only in this form he could overcome the enemy). It was considered essential to study animals to understand the mysteries of the universe or to gain magical powers. In Ayurveda it embraced the study of animals in sickness and the means of curing their ills. In ancient times many hospitals were established for the care of sick animals, birds, fishes and even insects. From earliest times - Indians were well known all over the world for training, breeding and care of elephants and horses. The crocodile is the vehicle of river goddess Ganga, as the tortoise of river of Goddess Yamuna. Sometimes crocodiles are kept in sacred tanks where they are worshipped. In mythology snub-nosed crocodile (magar) is known as a sea monster, which represents the Capricorn of the Hindu zodiac. It has the head and forelegs of a deer, and the body and tail of a fish. It is the vehicle of Varuna (deity which sustains universe) and also figures on the banner of Kama (god of love).

Birds, the study of their cries and behaviour constituted a science of its own. In Hindu mythology they are the messengers of the gods, have access to the celestial and infernal realms, and are the custodians of many secrets hidden from mankind. Serpents (especially, nag or cobra) have always been worshipped in some parts of India. Mystery of serpent knowledge is a tradition in some Hindu sects from time immemorial. Above all animals the cow was raised to a position of supreme sanctity and its milk, butter and yoghurt has always been held sacred. The bull has received veneration as a symbol of virility. The buffalo (vehicle of Yama - god of death) is now generally used for ploughing or drawing carts in place of oxen The buffalo demon was once slain by Devi (goddess) hence the buffalo is usually sacrificed to her especially in Nepal.

Antelope

Antelope, gazelle's skin is much in use among ascetics. Lord Shiva is supposed to wear it. In some parts of India, antelopes are not killed and many people worship them as well. The saint, Shring Rishi was born of a nymph transformed into a doe.

The Bull or Basava

This is the favourite deity of the Saivites or the followers of Lord Sivas. Hindus regard their cattle with extraordinary veneration, for as a matter of fact it would be difficult for them to live without their help. Therefore these animals are the most sacred objects of their religion. The image of Nandi, the bull if Siva, of a milky white colour, is to be found in every temple dedicated to Lord Siva. The sacred bull is usually represented as lying down on a pedestal, with three of his legs doubled under him, and the right forefoot extended straight beyond his head. He is the chamberlain of Lord Siva, chief of his personal attendants, and carries a staff of office. He is guardian of all four footed animal. The nations, which did not actually worship animals as gods, were always careful to show the high value they set upon them. For example, amongst the Romans to kill a bull was as serious a crime as killing a human being.

Conch (Shankh)

The shell of the Turbinella pyrum, is worshipped in front of the family gods. Shankh is said to be the brother of Lakshmi (the goddess of wealth and prosperity), because both of them were churned out of the ocean. Shankasur was the shell-demon, which Lord Vishnu killed in his first incarnation (Matsya). Vishnu and Krishna has a conch called Panchajanya and Arjuna has one called Devadatta.

Cow

The cow was considered a supreme sanctity, as its milk, butter and yoghurt are held to be sacred. In Hindu mythology the bovine species occupies a prominent place. In India cow and divine has always been very close to each other. Kamadhenu (A miraculous cow of plenty who could give her owner whatever he desired) and her daughter Surabhi were sacred cows. Lord Krishna is associated with cows and his paradise is called Goloka (cow-place). It was believed that cows were created on the same day as Brahma (creator) and that of sin of killing cow was heinous. Cow protection is the gift of Hinduism to the world. Mother cow gives us milk, butter and yoghurt and in return expects nothing except grass and grain.

Cowries

Shells (Cypress monita), used as coins in India, in Bengal are supposed to represent Lakshmi (the goddess of wealth and prosperity). They are worshipped along with Lakshmi. The goddess of Kolhapur wears a wreath of shells and her devotees do the same.

Fish

Matsya (fish) was the first incarnation of Vishnu to save the world. A fish is a lucky symbol. It is lucky to meet one carrying fish. It forebodes success.

Ganesh (Elephant headed god)

Elephant is considered auspicious and indicates royalty. Its association with Ganesh has made it sacred. Ganesh is Lord of Ganas (inferior deities), especially those attendant upon Lord Siva. He is the god of wisdom and remover of obstacles; hence he is invariably propitiated at the beginning of any important undertaking, and is invoked at the commencement of books. He is represented as a short fat man of a yellow colour, with a protuberant belly, four hands, and the head of an elephant, which has only one tusk. In one hand he holds a shell, in another discus, in the third a club or goad, and in the fourth a water lily. His temples are numerous all over India. There are a variety of reasons legends accounting for his elephant head. One is that his mother Parvati, wife of Lord Siva, went to her bath and told her son to keep the door. Lord Siva wanted to enter and was opposed, so he cut off Ganesh's head. To pacify Parvati he replaced it with an elephant's head, the first that came to hand. In some parts of India elephants are worshipped as Ganesh.

Garuda

It is a mythical bird or vulture, half-man, half-bird, on which Lord Vishnu rides. The bird is held in great honour, especially by the followers of Vishnu. He is the king of birds and a great enemy of serpents. His lustre was so brilliant that soon after his birth the gods mistook him for Agni (fire) and worshipped him. He is represented as having the head, wings, talon, and beak of an eagle and the body and limbs of a man. In some parts of South India Sunday is especially devoted to garuda worship.

Hanuman (Monkey-chief)

According to Hindu mythology Hanuman was a celebrated monkey-chief, son of Pavan (wind) and Anjana. He was able to fly, and is a conspicuous figure in Ramayana. He and other monkeys who assisted Lord Ram in his war against Ravanas were of divine origin, and their powers were super-human.

Monkeys are treated as sacred animals all over India as they helped Lord Rams to kill Ravana and save Sita from him. The greater part of Ramayana (story of Lord Ram) is devoted to the achievements and devotion of Hanuman and his soldiers to Lord Ram. The cult of monkey Hanuman extends all over the whole of India. The followers of Vishnu are especially devoted to this deity. Images of Hanuman are to be seen in most temples and most of the houses and public places. The offerings made to Hanuman are of natural products (boiled rice, fruit, nuts etc). This is considered a most meritorious act.

Nagas - Snakes

A snake, especially the cobra is believed to be a mythical serpent of semi-divine status. Snake-worship is very common in many parts of India and it may be possible that its origin is due to natural fear of these reptiles. They try to propitiate the poisonous species with offerings of food and milk. The Nag-panchami festival is celebrated in the beginning of February in honour of snakes, chiefly cobras. This snake is very common and the most dangerous of all, is honoured in a very special manner on this occasion. A popular story regarding the festival is that a Brahman had seven daughters-in-law. All of them used to go to their parents for holidays except the youngest whose parents had died. She told everyone that Nag king (Shesh-Nag snake) was her relation and protector. Shesh-Nag the thousand-hooded snake on whose coils sleeps Lord Vishnu, was moved to pity. He assumed the shape of an old Brahman and went to claim the girl as her niece. She spent her holidays with Shesh-Nag and his wife. On return to her husband's family she started praying to Shesh-Nag and became rich and happy. There are some temples erected in South and North India in their special honour.

Peacock

It is the charger of goddess Sarasvati (goddess of learning). It is also the charger of Kumar, the god of war, the six-headed son of Shiva. It is a sacred bird in India. Its feathers are largely used in making headdress ornaments - accepted as signs of royalty. Krishna had his headdress decorated with peacock's feathers.

Pig

The pig is considered sacred to Gauri (Goddess). Vishnu in his third incarnation appeared as a boar to save the world from the demon Hiranyaksha. King Ashoka in one of his pillar edicts declared that the rhinoceros to be sacred and no one was allowed to kill the animal.

Salagram

A stone held sacred and worshipped by the Vaishnavas, because its spirals are supposed to contain or to be typical of Vishnu. It is a fossiled shell, ammonite or nautilus. The more there are of these tree-like markings, the more highly they are revered. The fossiled shell was found in the river Ganges, and is valued more or less highly according to the number of spirals and perforations. Though the Salagram is looked upon as one of the metamorphoses of Vishnu, it partakes at the same time of the essence of all other deities, and through it worship can be offered to all of them. There is nothing more efficacious for the remission of sins than to possess some water in which the salagram has been washed. He who always keeps such water in his house ensures thereby perpetual wealth, good health and happiness in this world.

Sparrows are considered harbingers of harvest and are never killed by most of the Hindus.

Worship of Inanimate objects

The Egyptians worshipped onions and other products of their garden and similarly Hindus worshipped grass, trees, stone and a plant etc. In Hinduism there are three hundred and thirty million of deities whom they recognise and amongst the inanimate things they consider most sacred and worship the salagram stone, Tulsi plant, darbha grass, and the sacred fig tree.

Aghada (Achyranthes aspera)

This tree represents Gauri (Shiva's wife) in the absence of balsam. Its twigs are used as tooth-brushes on the Rishipancham day. In the Puran, called Chaturmas Mahatmaya, this plant is called the transformation of Buddha the 9th incarnation of Vishnu. Its twigs are required for the sacred fire. The leaves are used in Ganesh worship. It is a highly respected plant.

Am or Amb (Mangifera Indica)

Mango inflorescence is held sacred to the Moon, to whom it is offered on the second day of Magh. It is also sacred to Madan-the Indian Cupid. Festoons of mango leaves are hung at the door, round the halls and bowers in which marriage and other auspicious ceremonies are held. It is believed that this tree is the transformation of the god Prajapati. Its twigs are ordered to be used as tooth-brushes, and its leaves as spoons for pouring libations. On Maha-Shiv-Ratri day, Lord Shiva is worshipped with its blossom.

Apta (Bauhinea tomentosa)

It is worshipped and looted on Dussehra day and its leaves over which mantras (hymns or incantations) are repeated and distributed as gold. In Dharma Sindhu Puran it is recommended that in the absence of the Shami tree (Prosopis spicigera) must be worshipped on the Dussehra day.

Asoka (Jonesia Asoka or Saraca Indica)

This tree is held sacred on account of its association with the abduction of Sita (wife of Lord Ram) – who was kept in a garden containing groves of this tree. The buds of this tree are eaten by women in Bengal on the Asoka Shasthi Day. It is supposed to bloom tremendously if kicked by a young lady.

Bel or Bael (Aegle marmelos)

Its trifoliate leaf is sacred to Lord Shiva and the worship of the god is not complete without it. The Chaturmas Mahatmaya says that its three leaves represent the Hindu triad (Brahma, Vishnu and Shiva). The Jaimini Aranya Katha records that Draupadi the wife of Pandavas was ordered to offer a hundred thousand of the leaves of this tree to Shiva.

Cocoanut (Cocos nucifera)

The Sanskrit word for coconut (narikera or narikela) is of Austric (eastern Indian) origin, and the use of coconut in Hindu ceremonies is derived from prehistoric practice. There is a belief in Malabar that the tree was brought to India from Ceylon. It has a special significance for the Hindus as it provides food, drink and all other necessities of life. It is a symbol of fertility and is kept in temples for presentation to women who desire to become mothers. The coconut is closely associated with Shiva as its three 'eyes' symbolize the three-eyed god.

It is considered an auspicious offering to gods, and is worshipped as Lakshmi in the absence of an image. When placed on top of a water-pot, it represents the god of rain. It is believed that the cocoanut plant is the wish-granting tree of primitive society. Its stem supplies beams for cottages, or when scooped out it serves as a canoe. The leaves cover huts as roofs, the flower-stocks yield a cool drink, the fruit gives food, oil, and milk like juice, and the shell of the fruit yields medicinal oil and serves as a fuel. The husk supplies ropes for building huts, etc. In fact everything required for the nourishment and housing of a primitive society is supplied by this tree and therefore it is called wish-granting tree (Kalpa Vriksha). It is considered sacred in Hinduism and continues to be used in hundreds of Hindu ceremonies. In the simplest form a coconut is broken before an image and offered to the deity. It is auspicious and a sign of good luck to break a coconut in any Hindu ceremony. Ships are ceremonially launched by breaking a coconut on the bows instead of the Western style champagne bottle.

Dub (Cynodon dactylon)

Its leaves are sacred to Ganesh who is worshipped with them. The Chaturmas Mahatmaya says that this plant is the transformation of Rahu. It is worshipped on the eighth day of Bhadrapad (August-September). It is there said to be a very fertile and gregarious goddess and her marriage with the Ficus Indica is recommended.

Darbha Grass

The plant belongs to the genus borage. It is found in all damp marshy grounds. Many Hindus keep it in their houses, and it is used in all their ceremonies. It grows to the height of about two feet and is finally pointed at the top. It is believed that it was produced at the time when the gods and the demons were busy churning the sea of milk in order to obtain nectar (amrit) of immortality. The vessel containing the nectar was supported on Mohini's hips, from which some fleshy filaments fell, and taking root in the ground, developed under the form of Darbha grass. It is looked upon as part of Lord

Vishnun himself. On the strength of this it is worshipped because it possess the virtue of purifying everything. The grass is essential in all rituals for the welfare of people who uses it.

Fig Tree (Ficus-religious)

There are many different species of trees, which the Hindus consider sacred and accordingly worship. The fig tree comes first on the list. of sacred trees. The two chief varieties of the Indian fig tree are the banyan and the pipal. The banyan tree is one of the most beautiful trees in the country, and grows to a huge size. It is considered to possess health-giving properties. In Sanskrit it is called banyan tree, remarkable for its great spread of rooting branches, making it appear, as it were, a vast temple of the plant world. Milton in Paradise Lost describes it as having arms - branching so broad and long, that in the ground, the bended twigs take root and grow to the size of the original. It is believed that under this tree Lord Vishnu was born, therefore it is regarded with great respect and veneration. No one is allowed to cut it down, lop of its branches, or even pull of its leaves unless they are to be used for acts of worship. The tree is sacred to Lord Vishnu. At the end of every Yuga god lies down to rest on its leaf, which in fact has its branches everywhere. Allahabad and Gaya claim to have the tree in their cities, and they are supposed to exist from primordial times. It was under the shade of this tree that Lord Buddha received enlightenment; hence it is also referred to as the Bodhi or Bo tree.

The Pipal tree is worshipped for its association with the three gods (Brahma, Vishnu and Shiva). It is frequented by all gods and therefore it is very sacred. No one should fell it. Women should worship it, and go round it a thousand times in a day for health, wealth and prosperity of their family. In the Shravan Mahatmaya, it is ordained that this tree should be worshipped on every Saturday of the month of Shravan (July-August). Sage Valmiki tells us that Lord Vishnu resides in that. Its dry twigs are used in the worship of the sacred fire.

Neem (Melia Azardirachta)

Its leaves are eaten on the New year's day wherever it is available. Its medicinal properties are well known all over the world and are also recorded in India folklore. The oil of this tree is used for curing leprosy and skin diseases. During the epidemic of small pox, festoons of the fresh leaves of this tree are hung on the doors of all the Indians.

Plantain (Musa paradisiacal)

Some people claim the position of the all-wish-granting tree (cocoanut) to plantain. In many pujas (worship), bowers made up of four plantain trees used, as pillars are considered acceptable to gods. Women worship this for the long life and good health of their family. When placed near the entrances of houses along with its long leaves and laden with fruit, this tree forms an emblem of plenty and fertility.

Rui (Calotropis gigantia)

The leaves of this plant are offered to Mangal Gaur, and the wreath of the same is put round Hanuman's neck for the prosperity of one's family and friends. At a marriage, the bride for welcome and to bring happiness in their lives puts a garland of the flowers of this plant round the neck of bridegroom. In Skandapuran this tree is supposed to be the transformation of the sun. Its dried twigs are used in feeding the sacrificial fire.

Til (Sesamum indicum)

It is associated in Bengal with the worship of the goddess of wealth possibly due to its utility as a commercial product. The souls of the dead ancestors are worshipped with this seed. It is pounded and applied to the body on the Sakrant day. It is also coated and mixed with sugar and eaten on the same day. Its oil is used for cooking etc.

Tulsi (plant)

The Tulsi (Ocymum sanctum) plant is to be found everywhere in sandy and uncultivated places. It is a species resembling the basil that grows in Europe. It is believed that there nothing an equivalent to Tulsi, and worship must be offered to it daily. When a Hindu is dying a bit of leaf of Tulsi is placed in the mouth of the dying man, and he is then sprinkled from head to foot with the Tulsi twig — which has been dipped in water. The man then can die in certainty that he will go straight to heaven. By touching the plant a man can is purified from all defilement. By eating plant leaves, it is believed, that a person would be cured from some diseases. Salvation is assured to any one who waters and attends to it every day. If a branch of it is offered to Lord Vishnu in the month of November, it will be very pleasing to the god. Many Hindus cultivate the plant in their houses, and offer it daily prayers and sacrifices. The Tulsi is usually planted on a little mound of sand, which they call Vrinda-vanam, or on a square pillar, three or four feet in height, hollow at the top, with its four sides facing the four sides of the compass. Hindis consider it a meritorious act to carefully water and cultivate the plant.

Its leaves have a sweet aromatic scent and act as a cough elixir and cordial; indeed Hindus think that they possess many medicinal properties. Hindus always swallow one or two leaves of Tulsi after meals as an aid to digestion. Perhaps it is die to the medicinal qualities that the Hindus deified the plant in the first instant.

Ornaments worn by Hindus

Ornaments for the body have always been the passion of the people of India. Every Hindu, even including those who have made a profession of penitence and have renounced the world, wears earrings. The Sanyasis (pentinents) who has given up everything (honours, riches and women) wear copper earrings in token of humility. But generally such ornaments are made of gold, and are of different shapes, though most frequently oval. Ear ornaments, which are sometimes of enormous size, are another proof of the Hindu strong attachment to his ancestral customs. All writers, sacred and profane, bear witness to the fact that similar ornaments have been worn from time immemorial. On grand occasions, such as marriages, they put on four pairs into their ears, and at the end or in the centre of each of these is added another small ornament set with some precious stone. In some parts of the country a gold ring is also attached to the cartilage, which divides the nostrils. Poor people wear some small inexpensive trinket in their ears for adornment.

Rich Hindus wear round their necks gold chains or strings of pearls with large medallions set with diamonds, which reach to their chests, and also they wear gold finger-rings set with precious stones. Many women wear round their waists a girdle made of gold or silver thread woven with such taste and skill, and carry massive gold bracelets on their arms. Many women wear silver rings in their toes. Many people also tie above their elbows little hollow tubes of gold or silver containing magical mantras, which they wear as charms to avert ill luck. The variety and number of ornaments is almost bewildering; but they all have their proper names and shapes. There are no changing fashions, either in dress or in ornaments. A woman can wear what once belonged to her, or to one grandmother. There is a perpetual recurrence of old patterns and designs. There is a lot of variety in jewels for women. For women colour, brightness and design in decoration and in fashioning ornaments the metals used are always carefully planned. Usually a man's wealth was spent on his wife's ornaments, symbolised his fortune, and like a powerful talisman attracted auspicious forces. Three thousand year old necklaces, rings, amulets, bracelets, waistbands, nose-studs, earrings, set with precious stones have been found in Indus Valley. Rich Vedic Aryans, whose garments were also embroidered with gold, always used gold ornaments. Many Sanskrit writers name about seven hundred kinds of ornaments for men and women made of gold, silver, and mixed with metals, pearl and jewels, and shaped like flowers, butterflies, fishes, birds, and animals, or stars, crescents and flames.

Head ornaments included fillets and bands called kesa-bandh (hair band), often studded with gems; all classes wore these. The diadem or crest jewel or crown, were the insignia of royalty and nobility. In the medieval times a plume and sarpesh (turban ornament) was a headdress of Hindu chieftains. The forehead was adorned with an elaborate jewelled fringe or a string of small pearls. Some of them hung low over the forehead reaching to the cheeks. The neck was adorned with a necklace, multiple ropes of pearls or beads superbly worked neckbands, jewelled collars and pendants of intricate design. Earrings (kundalas), often very large and pendulous, or following the curve of the ear, and shaped like a snake, dragon or lion, were worn by both sexes. A nose ring (nathani) or stud is the most important insignia of many women. The shoulder ornaments of many kinds were worn, while the forearm had a band called the valaya. The wrist was covered with a thick bracelets often covered the whole forearm. Glass was made in India from ancient times, but Sanskrit writers until the eighth century does not refer to the use of glass for bangles, so common today. All used finger rings and thumb rings in all shapes and sizes. There were ornaments for thighs, heavy silver chain with tiny bells for ankles, so that a delicate tinkling is heard when the woman walks, and toe rings or jewelled studs for the toes of women.

Caste Marks

The tilak (mole), or tikka (spot) is a mark made on forehead, arms or chest, with red, yellow or white pigment, with sindhur (red lead), sandal wood paste or ashes, to designate one's caste. Tattooing was common in Patanjali's time (200 BC), and many women often had a star tattooed on the chin. After this period many married women began to make mark (tilak) on the forehead with red pigment as a sign of married woman. The Hindu devotee usually marks himself, with his sect mark. The marks may be horizontal or perpendicular lines, dots, rectangles, circles, oblongs or triangles. They are usually made on forehead, but more fervent devotees may have their insignia made on their shoulders, arms, stomach, and breast etc. Sometimes the caste mark is a more permanent seal. In such cases the design may be that of a conch shell, discuss, lotus, mace or some other symbol. Sect marks are generally divided into two main classes; those of the Vaishvanites (followers of Vishnu, Krishna and Ram), and those of Salivates (followers of Siva). Vaisavanite caste marks are usually perpendicular and include: a single perpendicular line; two vertical strokes either open or meeting below in a curve, with a dot in the middle, denoting the following of Vishnu. And called the urdhhva-pundra; three lines, one red perpendicular and two white at an incline meeting at the base and forming a sort of trident, and called the naman.mark; and also two perpendicular strokes meeting both above and below in an oval. Saivite marks are generally horizontal (two or three horizontal lines with a dot below or in the centre, made with white or grey ash and represent the half-moon on Siva's head drawn three times; also a triangle or half moon with a dot in the middle.

In South India there is the custom of painting the forehead and other parts of the body with different figures and emblems in various colours. The most common is called pottu, which consists of a small circular mark about an inch in diameter, placed in the centre of the forehead. It is usually yellow, but sometimes red or black in colour, and the paint is mixed with sweet smelling sandalwood powder. Instead of pottu (dot) somc paint two or three horizontal lines across their forehead to the nose. Some also decorate the neck, breast, belly, and arms with different designs. Many Hindus who do not belong to any sect smart their head with sandal paste or ashes.

7.

Pilgrimage

Lisiting holy places is one of the main religious duties of the Hindu. The place of pilgrimage is called Tirath (sacred spot or bathing place) worthy of reverence. There are many holy places in India, to which a pilgrimage may be undertaken. Some are of special sanctity for Saivites and some for Vaishnavites. Saivites pilgrimages are the sites where the great lingas are enshrined. Vaishnavvites go to places associated with Vishnu, Krishna and Ram. The pilgrimage also include the seven holy cities of Ayodha, Mathura, Gaya, Banaras, Ujjain, Hardwar, Dwarka; the seven sacred rivers (Ganges, Jamna, Saraswati, Godavari, Narmada, Indus, and Kaveri); sacred hills and mountains (Kailas, Parasnath, Girnar, Mount Abu, Palni and others); also holy lakes Sarovar), Mansarovar at the foot of Mount Kailas, the Puskar lake near Ajmere (sacred to Barhma).

According to Hindu belief there are several pilgrimage centres in India, but the four such centres are most sacred abodes, which are known as *Char Dham (four sacred abodes)* These are Badrinath (Uttaranchal), Puri (Orissa), Dwarka (Gujrat), and Rameshwaram (Tamil Nadu). For devout Hindus the attainment of moksha (liberation from the cycle of birth and death) is the prime purpose in life and a visit to these four places is believed to lead to moksha (salvation).

There are special priests who will assist the pilgrim at the important places of pilgrimage. The pilgrim usually makes a purifying bath in the sacred river or lake, worship the idol and gives presents to the priest etc. An important part of all pilgrimage is the circumambulation, in which the worshipper walks several times around the idol or temple. The merit of pilgrimage is enhanced if the pilgrim adds difficulties to his progress. Today the railways and aeroplanes have shortened the time spent on pilgrimage.

8.

Mantra

In the Vedic literature the Mantras are those portions that consist of the metrical psalms of praise. They constitute the main body of the Vedic collection, and are the most ancient part of the sacred writings. Originally any Vedic hymn, which had to be recited by the priests for a particular purpose, was called Mantra. Later a Mantra was also known as a hymn, which the teacher gives to his pupil to meditate on, for fruitful and good life or for some particular gain. Mantras were sometimes revealed to the sages by direct inspiration, but they composed many after long meditation on the mysteries of sound, by means of which they were able to reduce voluminous doctrines to small compass. Every Hindu ritual has its own prescribed Mantras appropriate for the occasion, and great stress is laid on the proper recitation of Mantras.

The results produced by Mantras are varied. Some bring mystic trance and some enlightenment and many other benefits. It is believed that by chanting a Mantra correctly, a god could be compelled to fulfil the wishes of the devotee. Mantras are divided as (1) Kanthak (throated), which give expression to, by the voice, and Bhramara (humming). (2) Ajapa (non-uttered), Mantras that are not spoken but repeated internally. Calling out the names of one deity is held to be amongst the most powerful of Mantras. Thus a Saivite will recite the 1008 names of Siva in the belief that such repetition will procure the god's blessings. Vaisvanite also believe that by uttering the name of Vishnu one will go to heaven. Finally, since the Vedic hymns were believed to have magic power, Mantras can mean magic formulas, which work wonders.

The intellectual well being of the child was very important and the hymns uttered on this occasion were symbolical of intelligence; they were recited with the great *Gayatri Mantra:*

Om Bhur Bhuvah Svaha Tat Savitu Varenyam Bhargo Devasya Dhimahi Dhiyo Yo Nah Prachodyaat.

Om (means Brahma, Vishnu, Mahesh) *Bhur* (earth) *Bhuvah* (sky) *Svaha* (heaven) *Tat* (the essence) *Savitu* (the creator – divine light – sun) *Varenyam* (is worth worshipping) *Bhargo Devasya Dhimahi* (upon the glory we meditate) *Dhiyo Yo Nah Prachodyaat* (the intellect which us may guide).

It means – let us meditate on the most excellent light of the Creator (the divine Sun); may the Almighty guide our intellect and illuminate our minds.

The substances, with which the child was fed, were also conducive to mental health. The father with his fourth finger and an instrument of gold gave to the child honey and ghee (clarified butter). The formula employed, "Bhuh Bhuvah Svah or Bhur bhuvah svah (I put into your mouth everything good for your intellect and well being).

Gunas (Quality)

The term Guna is of very wide application, and is extensively in many branches of Hindu learning. Vaishesika philosophy lists twenty-four kinds of Gunas of which sixteen are inherent in material substances and eight are inherent in the soul. The sixteen Guunas inherent in substance are colour, taste, smell, sound, touch, number, extension, individuality, conjunction, disjunction, priority, posteriority, weight, fluidity, viscidity, and self-reproduction. The eight Gunas inherent in the soul are: knowledge, volition, desire, aversion, pleasure, pain, merit and demerit.

In Sankhya philosophy Guna means three principles of nature: Sattasva (goodness, light, truth, fruits, serenity), Rajas (passion, aggressiveness), and Tamas (darkness, untruth, stale food, sloth).

The Gunas exist in all individuals in varying degrees, and owing to the attachments to them the embodied soul is bound in nature as slave. If Sattava (goodness) is the predominating Guna in a man he goes to celestial realms after death, if Rajas (passion) he is born as a man., if Tamas (darkness) he reincarnates as a lower animal. .

9.

The Astrology, Palmistry and Horoscope

From the time of the Vedas (10,000 BC) astrology (jyotisha) has always been very close to Indian life, and many people usually consult a fortune-teller for advice on daily life. Many people consult astrologers regarding jobs, passing examinations, getting married, regarding illnesses, birth of a child and other important issues one may face in life. Tradition makes it obligatory to seek the service of an astrologer in respect of the twenty-one ceremonies, starting from the pre-natal period of the child, which orthodox Hindus are expected to perform on auspicious dates and times fixed according to fixed astrological considerations. The auspicious times is required for naming the child, putting him/her on solid food, for beginning its schooling, for the child's first hair-cut, for religious initiation, marriage, consummation of marriage, wife's going to her parents home for her first confinement, have all to be decided in consultation with the astrologer. In marriage astrology plays an important role. In arranged or love marriage the horoscopes of the boy and girl are shown to the astrologer as to how far they match and complement each other. The time of birth of the boy and the girl is enough to assess their affinity to each other in matters of health, fitness, sex, marital loyalty and temperament. It also detects whether their union would be fruitful in longevity, wealth and children. There is no divorce in Hinduism except in rare circumstances. The solar and lunar eclipse times, the new moon, eighth day after the new moon are regarded unlucky for weddings, applying for new jobs, building a house, digging a well, sowing seeds and ploughing the first furrow in the fields. Then there are auspicious times when one is asked to start treatment when one is seriously ill. Each birth in the world takes place under one or other of the 27 asterisms mentioned in the astrology books. On this basis each person has his own birth-tree, birth-animal, and birth-bird besides his/her own birth star. One is warned not to destroy one's birth-tree, or injure the birth-animal, or birth-bird. It pleases the stars if one nurtures them carefully. Hinduism believes in Karma (deeds or action). The horoscope indicates a man's karma (action) or past deeds, which is a blueprint of his destiny in the present life. The main purpose of astrology is to discover the effects of one's past actions (karma) and to mitigate the bad in them by good actions in this life to one's advantage. There is perpetual tug-of-war between destiny and free will. A person of superior will force, or high spiritual attainments, can change his destiny by his good actions.

Horoscopes are usually written with calculations made from the date and time of birth of a person actually born. Another branch of fortune telling is called Prasana Marg (question method). The fortune-teller sits with a picture of ruling planetary position in his mind. The time of consultation, the first letter uttered and some other indications enable him to guess the questions. A refined form of Prasana Marg (question method). is also called Doota Lakshana (telepathy), in which a client need not utter a word. Palmistry is also a very popular method of fortune telling. It is claimed that margin of error is far less in palmistry than in horoscopy. Thumb reading is also very popular in south India. The art is successful in detecting internal troubles and mental diseases. Another set of fortune-tellers base their predictions on reading the limbs of a person. A practitioner would look at the forehead, tell the asterism under which he was born and read his fortune as if from a book.

10.

Symbolism

The representation of an object or being by a symbol or emblem related to it in some way is very common in Hinduism. The animal plant and mineral worlds provide symbols of deep esoteric significance. Most of the important symbols are to be found in legends connected with the deities. In pictorial representations, the gods are known with their traditional insignia and bearings. In mythology the deities are described in association with their symbols, such as weapons, animal vehicles. Every deity has its appointed consort, offspring, sacred cites, jurisdiction, names and titles, incarnation, animal mounts, auspicious bodily marks, weapons, musical instruments, colours, flowers, dress, jewels and ornaments etc. Here are some of the prominent Hindu symbols:

Aum/Om

This most sacred symbol represents creation and Hindu triad (Brahma, Vishnu, Shiva). It is the root syllable of origination and dissolution. It is used at the commencement of prayers, religious ceremonies, and placed at the beginning of books.

Jyoti (light)

It represents an atmosphere of purity, serenity and calm, and signifies the sun and fire without which life is impossible. It is lit in every temple and prayer room of Hindu homes.

Natraj

This symbolizes Shiva, the Lord of Dance. The circle around the dancing figure represents the continuity of the life cycle.

Saffron flag

It signifies the house of god or a temple, and stands for purity, devotion and godliness. Holy men wear saffron clothes to signify their attachment to god and the spiritual path.

Shankh (Conch shell)

It signifies the origin of universe from a single source (i.e. Brahman – One Supreme God) and water from which the universe evolved. The sound it produces when blown, represents the primeval sound of Om, which marked the beginning of creation. Shankh is said to be the brother of Lakshmi (the goddess of wealth and prosperity), because both of them were churned out of the ocean. Shankasur was the shell-demon, which Lord Vishnu killed in his first incarnation (Matsya). Vishnu and Krishna has a conch called Panchajanya and Arjuna has one called Devadatta.

Swastika

It is a symbol of good luck, happiness, prosperity and world peace. It represents divinity and the four directions (north, south, east and west) of the universe. It also signifies four Vedas and four seasons (spring, summer, autumn and winter.

Symbolism - see: Worship of animals and Worship of inanimate objects.

Bibliography

Avasthi, Asha. Hindu marriage in continuity and change. Lucknow, 1979.

Basham, A.L.A cultural history of India. London, 1974.

Balfour, Edward. The cyclopaedia of India and of Eastern and Southern Asia. London, 1885. 3 Vols.

Bhavani, Enakshi. The dance in India: the origin and history, foundations, the art and science of the dance in India – classical, folk and tribal. Bombay, 1965.

Braddock, Joseph. The bridal bed. London, Robert Hale Limited,1960.

Chatterjee, C. K. Studies in the rites and rituals of Hindu marriage in ancient India. New Delhi, 1978.

Derraugh, Pat and Bill. Wedding etiquette. London, Foulsham, 1998.

Dowson, John. Classical dictionary of Hindu Mythology, religion, geography, history and religuion. London, Routledge, 1957.

Dogra, Ramesh C. and Urmila. Hindu and Sikh wedding ceremonies. Delhi, 2000.

Dogra, Ramesh C. and Urmila. Hinduism. Delhi and London, 2003.

Dogra, Ramesh C. and Urmila. India the land of wonders. Delhi & London, 2006.

Dogra, Ramesh C. and Urmila. The Sikh world: An encyclopaedic survey of Sikh religion and culture. Delhi. 2003.

Dogra, Ramesh C. and Urmila. Thought provoking Hindu names. Delhi 1999.

Dubois, A. J. A. Hindu manners, customs and ceremonies. Oxford, 1906.

Farquhar, J. N. The crown of Hinduism. Oxford, OUP, 1913.

Gupta, Rai Bahadur. Hindu holidays and ceremonies. Calcutta, Thacker, 1916.

Knappert, Jan. Indian mythology. London, Diamond Books, 1991.

Kanitkar, V. P. (Hemant) and Cole. W.O. Hinduism . London, 1995

Kapadia, K. M. Marriage and family in India. Bombay, 1955.

Kearns, J.F. Marriage ceremonies of the Hindus of South India. Madras, 1868.

Knappert, Jan. Indian mytholopgy: an encyclopaedia of myth and legend. London, Diamond Books, 1995.

Menski, W. F. Change and continuity in Hindu marriage rituals, London, 1991.

Mishra, Srikant. Ancient Hindu marriage law and scriptures. New Delhi, 1994.

Mitra, Ved. Happy married life in ancient India. New Delhi, 1965.

Modi, J. J. Symbolism in the marriage ceremonies of different nations. Bombay, Caxton Printing, 1909.

Pandey, R. B. Hindu Samskaras. Banaras, 1949.

Radhakrishnan, S. The Hindu view of life. London, 1927.

Sarkar, R. N. Hindu marriage Act. New Delhi, 1956.

Sastri, A. M. Marriage forms under ancient Hindu law. Bombay, 1906.

Sastri, N. Hindu fasts and ceremonies, Madras, 1903.

Sengupta, N. Evolution of Hindu marriage with special reference to rituals. Bombay, 1965.

Stutley, Margaret and James. A dictionary of Hindiusm. London, Routl;edge, 1977. .

Walker, Benjamin. Hindu world: an encyclopedic survey of Hinduism. 2 vols. London, George Allen & Unwin, 1968.

Index